THE FACE OF VIRGINIA

LEE STATUE, RICHMOND

CAPITOL BUILDING, WILLIAMSBURG

SHENANDOAH VALLEY FROM SKYLINE DRIVE

THE FACE OF VIRGINIA

A. AUBREY BODINE

Honorary Fellow of the Photographic Society of America
Fellow of the National Press Photographers

Bonanza Books, New York

PURSE NETTERS OUT OF HORN HARBOR

This edition is published by Bonanza Books,
a division of Crown Publishers, Inc.
by arrangement with Bodine & Associates, Inc.
a b c d e f g h
BONANZA 1980 EDITION

Manufactured in the United States of America

Library of Congress Cataloging in Publication Data

Bodine, A Aubrey, 1907–1970.
    The face of Virginia.

    Includes index.
    1. Virginia—Description and travel—1951–
—Views. I. Title.
[F227.B6 1980]   917.55'04'4   79-24322
ISBN 0-517-30947-5

FOREWORD

AUBREY BODINE has been a friend of mine for more than twenty years, during which time I have watched him develop from a facile photographer of news to a philosophical recorder of man and nature. This volume is a fascinating illustration of the complete range of his remarkable abilities.

For instance, Bodine the newsman could not resist the humor of a "Welcome to Virginia" road sign, complete with painted dogwood blossoms, half-seen through a blinding snowstorm (page 125). Nor was he so over-awed by the creator of the University of Virginia that he avoided taking a picture of the statue of Mr. Jefferson with a robin on its head (page 106). Neither of these pictures constitutes great photography, but they provide refreshing wit in such a book.

More photogenic but equally accurate are Bodine's views of Virginia's economy. The ancient agricultural rite of cultivating tobacco has never been more handsomely recorded than in the field at Barnesville (page 142); the profusion and hurry of industry is everywhere indicated at the Covington paper mill (page 133); and the elegant ease of today's and tomorrow's tourism is reflected in the sweeping terraces of the Dulles Airport (page 108).

Bodine obviously feels the drama of history, and is remarkably adept in selecting exactly the right moment to make his photographs of Virginia's storied sites. The three ships at Jamestown have apparently just emerged from the mists of the Old World into the dawn of the New (page 23). VMI cadets seem to be passing in review before a Confederate general as they march into the setting sun of a lost cause (page 124). The excitement of the Atomic Age is somehow achieved in the departure of the *Enterprise* from her birthplace at Newport News (page 36).

But Bodine the artist is most seen in his pictures of the landscape. There is a wonderful communion between nature and this man, enabling him miraculously to present the essence of a particular site in photographic form. The glassy calm and vast horizontality of Virginia's Chesapeake Bay are summed up in his view near Whitestone (page 56). The undulating Piedmont country, with the rich pattern of fields and woods against distant hills, is brilliantly caught in his shot along Route 42 (page 136). I know of no more magnificent rendering of a storm over the Blue Ridge mountains than his poetic view from the Skyline Drive (page 132).

This book of pictures of Virginia is not another "historic shrines" review—though, of necessity, such oft-repeated shots are included. Nor is it a Chamber of Commerce boast, nor a sociologist's dissecting of an old State. It is, in fact, *The Face of Virginia* in all its aspects, as recorded by a tremendously able and sensitive photographer.

Now, enough of words; look at the pictures!

LESLIE CHEEK, JR.
Director Emeritus, Virginia Museum of Fine Arts

Marye's Heights, Fredericksburg

THE FACE IS TO THE FUTURE

By Virginius Dabney

VIRGINIA is Jamestown and Williamsburg, Yorktown and Appomattox. It is Pickett's Charge and the Valley of the Shenandoah, the beleaguered Capital of the Confederacy and the mist-shrouded peaks of the Alleghenies. It is the liner United States and the nuclear-powered carrier Enterprise sliding down the ways at Newport News, the hum of machinery in textile, steel and aluminum mills, the Museum of Fine Arts at Richmond and the Barter Theatre at Abingdon.

Virginia is blue mountains and sandy beaches, antique shrines and bloodsoaked battlefields, seats of learning and repositories of history, tobacco farms and apple orchards, dogwood trees and trumpet vines, goobers and sorghum, chiggers and poison ivy, buttermilk biscuit and cracklin' bread.

Virginia is a rich blend of forward-looking believers in the future and backward-looking believers in the past. It includes imaginative business men and industrialists as well as incisive intellectuals, talented painters and able writers. On the other hand, there are Virginians who are so bemused by the state's pristine glories that they can think of practically nothing else.

Virginia's overall political and social orientation is admittedly conservative by latter-day standards, and among its citizens are a small minority who seem to be mainly concerned with their own genealogy. But the Virginia of today is predominantly alert and enterprising. The stuffy, backward and reactionary commonwealth which a few critics have attempted to depict, exists no longer, if, indeed, it ever did. The wryly amusing saying that "most Virginians revere the past, deplore the present and mistrust the future" has lost just about any validity it ever had.

Virginia is one of the wealthiest of the Southern states, both per capita and in total output of manufactured goods and farm products. Its economy is prevailingly sound and well balanced, its government is honest and its cultural attitudes are encouraging.

Much is heard, both inside and outside the Old Dominion, of the "Byrd machine," long dominated by the late Senator Harry F. Byrd. This political mechanism is not without blemishes; it has stood, at times, athwart the path of progress, and it has steamrollered those who got in its way. But there are widespread misunderstandings with respect to the Byrd "organization," as it is termed by its admirers and adherents.

During the more than 35 years it has been in the ascendant, Virginia made progress in many directions.

In race relations, Virginia's record is better than that of most Southern states. An era of "massive resistance" to the U.S. Supreme Court's sweeping school decision of 1954 was in fact hardly more than a delaying action. Informed observers realized that these legal maneuvers could not be continued indefinitely, but they were convinced that time had to be bought somehow, in order to permit adjustment to tremendous social change. True, certain episodes were humiliating to those who valued the good name of the state—notably the complete shutdown of the public schools in Prince Edward County for several years. Once the courts of last resort had spoken, the commonwealth yielded reluctantly but quietly. Yet the Old Dominion received far fewer accolades than other states which behaved no better, but from which, perhaps, less was expected.

As long ago as 1947, the University of Virginia set a precedent for the South by permitting its football team to play Harvard at Charlottesville with a Negro in the Harvard lineup. The Virginia team voted unanimously in favor of the contest, and the game went off smoothly. Once more the gentlemanly traditions of Virginia had prevailed.

Virginia, needless to say, no longer occupies the pinnacle in the American scheme of things that she occupied a century and a half ago. Once the largest and most populous state among thirteen, the Old Dominion is now one state of average size among fifty, with only average influence. The breakaway of West Virginia during the Civil War was, of course, an important factor in reducing the state's size and population.

H. L. Mencken took note in 1920 of Virginia's slide down the toboggan, and evoked howls and imprecations from every corner of the commonwealth. In his blistering essay, "The Sahara of the Bozart", which characteristically described the whole South as an intellectual vacuum, the Gentleman With the Meat-Ax wrote:

"Consider the present estate and dignity of Virginia—in the great days indubitably the premier American state, the mother of Presidents and statesmen, the home of the first American university worthy of the name, the *arbiter elegantiarum* of the western world. Well, observe Virginia today. It is years since a first-rate man, save only [James Branch] Cabell, has come out of it;

U.S.S. Enterprise in the James River

it is years since an idea has come out of it. The old aristocracy went down the red gullet of war; the poor white trash are now in the saddle. . . A Washington or a Jefferson, dumped there by some act of God, would be denounced as a scoundrel and jailed overnight. Elegance, *esprit,* culture? Virginia has no art, no literature, no philosophy, no mind or aspiration of her own. . . . In brief, an intellectual Gobi or Lapland. Urbanity, *politesse,* chivalry? It was in Virginia that they invented the device of searching for contraband whiskey in women's underwear. . . ."

Usquebaugh is no longer sought in such bizarre Virginia locales as that mentioned by Mencken—in part, no doubt, because the stuff has been legalized. Moreover, the description which the caustic Marylander gave of the state, as of 1920, was not accurate, even then. Allowance must be made for the customary Menckenesque hyperbole.

But Mencken's exaggerations are far more obvious today than they were when the third decade of the century dawned. Virginia, in this year of grace, does have an art and a literature, as well as a philosophy, and it also has a mind and aspiration of its own.

Explanations for Virginia's lack of progress in the late nineteenth and early twentieth centuries usually revolved about the Civil War and its larcenous aftermath, laughingly called "reconstruction." The Old Dominion suffered more than any other Southern State in the conflict of the sixties. Many more important battles were fought on Virginia soil than in any other comparable area of the Confederacy, wide regions of the state were devastated by the Northern armies, and much of Richmond went up in flames at the close. True, reconstruction was considerably less severe here than in various other states farther to the South, a fact which compensated Virginia in some measure for the greater degree of wreckage which the commonwealth suffered during the fighting. (Virginia is one of four states entitled to the designation "commonwealth," by virtue of the fact that these states have officially termed themselves such. The other commonwealths are Massachusetts, Pennsylvania and Kentucky.)

Whatever the validity of the argument in days agone that Virginia's progress had been retarded by the war and the hard years that followed, the state stands on its own feet today. Nearly a century has passed since Appomattox and almost as long a period since reconstruction was brought to a close.

OAK SPRING, PAUL MELLON ESTATE, UPPERVILLE

The fact that Virginia is the oldest American state has somehow become obscured by the lush verbiage found in history books from the pens of overenthusiastic New Englanders. These zealous worshippers at the shrine of the Pilgrims succeeded over a long period in either forgetting all about Jamestown, playing dead when Jamestown was mentioned, or creating the impression that the year 1620 antedated the year 1607. The net result was that the meeting of the first legislative body in the new world—the Virginia General Assembly, which convened at Jamestown in 1619, the year before the Mayflower sailed from England—was left out of many school books. So was the fact that the English common law was brought to these shores in 1607, firmly incorporated in the Virginia colony's first charter.

Let it be freely conceded, however, that some formidable myths have grown up about the fair name of Virginia. One of these has to do with the origins of the state's "First Families." A good many of these "F.F.V.'s" would like you to believe that they are descended from the English Cavaliers. As a matter of fact, a mere handful are able to produce evidence of such ancestry; the vast majority are sprung from the English merchant class. In this there is of course nothing to be ashamed of, but the record should be kept straight.

Virginia admittedly has as aristocratic a tradition as any other state. Its principal rivals in this regard are probably Massachusetts and South Carolina. But the Bay State has never been ravaged by war, which means that the more blue-blooded denizens of Boston and Salem have at no time been reduced to the pathetic poverty that overtook the planters of Virginia and South Carolina after Appomattox. Some of these planters' descendants are sunk in penury, even today, with pillared mansions crumbling about them, and once-productive acres abandoned to broomsedge and pines.

Yet there is in Virginia a sufficient residue of vigorous, competent and honest heirs of the early colonists to give this commonwealth a record in the public service that is, in some respects, unsurpassed. The ultraconservative nature of the modern political tradition in Virginia is admitted, the great power of the dominant Democratic political organization is acknowledged. But no state in the Union has more incorruptible officeholders, and none is more free of demagogues.

The late Dr. George H. Denny, president of Wash-

GLEBE CHURCH, ON THE LOWER JAMES AT DRIVERS

ington and Lee University and later of the University of Alabama, once remarked: "It is a tradition that Virginia's motto 'Old Virginny Never Tires' is to be traced to the fact that Virginia habitually refuses to move fast enough ever to get tired."

Dr. Denny didn't elucidate. The causes of Virginia's leisurely tempo are not altogether obvious. They are to be found, in part, in the Anglo-Saxon conservatism of the state and its people. They lie, also, in the penchant of the controlling Democratic political organization for moving no faster than public opinion induces or forces it to move.

The "organization" has been wedded to the pay-as-you-go principle of financing improvements ever since a young man named Harry F. Byrd successfully led the fight against a $50,000,000 road bond issue back in 1923. This refusal to incur state debt was widely accepted for some time, and it unquestionably had much to do with the state's continuing fiscal solidity. But doubts have been creeping in of late, and the notion is

growing that pay-as-you-go has been elevated to the status of a sacred cow, and that some modifications are in order. This pay-as-you-go shibboleth accounts, in part, for the lack of progress in certain directions.

But Virginia is going forward dramatically today, especially in education, as a result of the adoption of a sales tax. Mental hospitals, highways and recreation also are moving ahead. As for the state's welfare program, Virginia has the doubtful distinction of being at or near the bottom of all the states with respect to per capita expenditures for old-age assistance, aid to dependent children and the blind, and general relief. This low rank is accounted for, in part, by the conservatism of the state government, and the conviction of its leaders that there has been so much chiseling in the welfare program that temptation to get on the rolls should be held to a minimum. There is also the feeling, which may also have some basis, that Virginians are proud, and that most of them would rather stand on their own feet than seek governmental assistance.

The well-mannered and stem-winding Virginia Democratic machine has had no truck with the roughneck tactics of a Pendergast gang or a Hague mob. It was led for many years by the able and impeccable Senator Harry F. Byrd, who was so sincere in feeling that no Senator had a right to accept benefits under a law which he voted for, that he actually refused all federal soil conservation payments for his orchards—some $200,000 in all. He also refused to sell a single apple to the government from the 200,000 Byrd-owned trees.

The dominant Democrats of the Old Dominion are generally suave, well-tailored and personable. The rise of a Huey Long, a Tom Heflin or a Theodore Bilbo to a position of political power in the state is unthinkable. The Byrd organization has always prided itself on the integrity of its operatives, and the dignity with which its Governors, Senators and Representatives comport themselves. True, county elections have been stolen occasionally. Absent voter frauds have occurred in limited areas of the state, and illegal bloc payments of poll taxes have been made in substantially the same areas. But nobody can recall even a charge that any member of the Virginia legislature has been so much as offered a bribe—much less that one has been accepted. Thiev-eries or other similar derelictions on the part of state officials are so rare as to be practically unknown.

This record of honesty in office unquestionably has had a good deal to do with the ability of the "organization" to remain in power. Another reason has lain in the fact that it has had extremely capable leadership, and has revealed an uncanny ability to stay one jump ahead of public sentiment. Senator Byrd and his cohorts have been almost supernatural in their appraisal of popular trends. When Mr. Byrd came into office as Governor in 1926, he promptly put through the General Assembly a reorganization of the state government, in the interests of economy and efficiency, making a record which attracted national attention. Had he not done so, he and his wing of the Democratic Party might have found themselves out of office at the end of his term. But his progressive record—which included passage of the strongest anti-lynching bill ever enacted in this country—served to calm the rumblings. It was not until a decade later that the mutterings of the dissidents reached such proportions as to require further prayerful attention. At that time, James H. Price, the only anti-machine Governor since 1922, was in office, and the voters were becoming restive.

REDDISH KNOB, GEORGE WASHINGTON NATIONAL FOREST

CRAB POTTER, CHESAPEAKE BAY

Governor Price advocated a series of progressive reforms, most of which were badly needed, but the "organization"-dominated General Assembly slaughtered his program. Then, at the end of his term, the "organization" backed able Representative Colgate W. Darden Jr. (later president of the University of Virginia) as Price's successor. He was triumphantly elected. The Assembly then proceeded to pass several of the reform measures which Governor Price had seen cut to pieces by that same legislative body. The revolutionary rumblings were quieted. Such are the ways of politics, even in Virginia.

While the "organization" has given the commonwealth conspicuously honest government, too many people are on the state payroll—a condition by no means limited to the Old Dominion. The first comprehensive study of the state's governmental machinery in two decades was made by a legislative commission in the late 1940's, and there were a few eliminations and consolidations. But much remains to be done.

There is undoubted political apathy in Virginia, and the vote is one of the lowest in the Union. This is due, in part, to a fairly widespread feeling of satisfaction with the existing situation. Then there is the fact that the Byrd "organization" has dominated the scene to such an extent that opposition has been futile most of the time. In mountainous Southwest Virginia, where there is a well-established tradition of intense Democratic-Republican rivalry, the people turn out in large numbers, but in most other areas participation is extremely low.

Another explanation for the relatively small turnout at the polls is that federal elections and state and local elections never occur in the same year. A further explanation is that Virginia has the "short ballot"—regarded as an extremely progressive move when it was adopted under Governor Harry Byrd, and still a desirable reform. Under it only three state officials (the Governor, Lieutenant-Governor and Attorney-General) are elected by popular vote. It appeared for years that the poll tax kept the vote down markedly, but of late this has seemed less of a factor.

The Republican Party is growing steadily in Virginia, and its upsurge should stimulate popular interest. As in the rest of the South, the two-party system is making an appeal to those who feel that Dixie has been too long "in the bag." The elections of November, 1966, signaled a "great leap forward" on the part of the GOP below the Potomac. Four of Virginia's ten Congressional districts went Republican. The shade of that great Democrat, Thomas Jefferson, must have stirred uneasily.

On the other hand, Jefferson would rejoice over the progress of his greatly cherished brainchild, the University of Virginia. Its schools of law and medicine

MORNING CATCH, TANGIER ISLAND

continue to be outstanding, its graduate school of business administration is a valuable addition, its accomplishments in scientific realms are noteworthy, and its library has the finest collection in existence of original manuscripts and early editions in the field of American literature. The newly-established University Press of Virginia provides a badly needed outlet for scholarly publication for the entire state.

But the Old Dominion has numerous other important institutions of higher learning. Virginia Polytechnic Institute is known for the quality and diversity of its courses in the various branches of engineering, so vital today, and now has more students in business administration than in agriculture. Virginia Military Institute, with its glorious traditions revolving about such names as "Stonewall" Jackson and George C. Marshall, continues to train young men whose leadership and courage in times of national danger have always been a

priceless heritage. The ancient College of William and Mary is developing remarkably as a center of the liberal arts. The Medical College of Virginia is renowned in its field.

A partial list of the privately-financed centers of the higher learning would necessarily include such fine old institutions for men as Washington & Lee, Hampden-Sydney and Randolph-Macon, each of which ranks in the first thirty educational institutions in the entire United States in the percentage of alumni listed in "Who's Who in America." In fact, Hampden-Sydney led the entire nation in this regard in 1930. Ten years later, Randolph-Macon was third in the nation and Hampden-Sydney fourth.

Among women's colleges, Virginia has three of the best to be found anywhere in Randolph-Macon Woman's College, Sweet Briar and Hollins.

Excellent educational facilities for Negroes are offered at publicly supported Virginia State and privately-financed Hampton Institute, Virginia Union University and St. Paul's College.

Virginia has always had exceptionally fine private preparatory schools. One of these, the Episcopal High School near Alexandria, goes back to 1839. Others, founded more recently, also are of the highest caliber, including Woodberry Forest near Orange, and St. Christopher's, St. Catherine's and Collegiate, all in Richmond.

On another level of society, in the poorer rural regions, far from the halls of learning, there are fewer Jeeter Lesters than one might assume to exist, on the basis of the horrendous picture drawn in "Tobacco Road." Such moronic degenerates as Jeeter are more numerous in the Deep South than in Virginia, more likely to be found in the cotton states than in the tobacco states—although "Tobacco Road" is a definite overstatement for both regions. But tenancy and share-cropping are less prevalent where the golden leaf is grown and harvested and the incredible and largely incomprehensible voice of the auctioneer yammers over the land.

Statistically, Virginia stands up well with respect to farm tenancy. Its figure of 14.4 per cent is far below that for the Carolinas, each of which has a percentage in excess of 30, and much superior to Georgia's 24.

Virginia tobacco is, of course, world famous—which makes all the more poignant the confession that North Carolina grows it in far larger volume than the state which gave it birth. Kentucky also out-produces the Old Dominion, and North Carolina exceeds it in tobacco manufacture.

However, Virginia is fortunate in its agricultural and industrial diversity. In contrast to states which concentrate on one or two gigantic crops or one or two great industries, Virginia has a number of each.

Most of Virginia's farm income is derived from three principal sources, which are virtually equal in the revenue they produce. These are cattle raising and dairying, with the beef critters feeding on the rolling pastures of the Southwest, the Piedmont and the Shenandoah Valley, and the dairy barns divided largely between Northern Virginia and the Valley; chicken and turkey farming, heavily concentrated in the Valley and on the Eastern Shore; and tobacco growing, with the important flue-cured crop raised in a belt of Southside Virginia counties near the North Carolina line, the dark-fired and sun-cured in Central Virginia, and the burley in the Southwest. The apples of the Valley, which form the core of the annual Winchester Apple Blossom Festival, and those of the Piedmont, go to make up the largest apple crop of any Southern state, and are substantial revenue producers. So are the hogs and peanuts of the Smithfield ham belt in lower Tidewater, where the porkers munch the peanuts and straightway acquire

a special flavor. Wheat and corn, grown in various sections, also are significant.

Virginia is no longer preponderantly rural. As recently as 1900, the rural percentage was more than 85, but by 1930 it had fallen to slightly in excess of two-thirds. Today the rural percentage is considerably less than half.

Farm mechanization has caused thousands to leave the farms for the cities of this and other states, with the result that many counties are losing population. This condition prevails widely throughout the nation.

In Virginia, important changes have flowed from this situation. Most of those who remain in the country districts are living better and operating larger farms. And thanks to the automobile, they tend to be *en rapport* with the *divertissements* of the cities. Some may regard this last as a sure sign that Virginia civilization has hit the toboggan for keeps, but others take the view that the change signifies a clear cultural advance.

The state is becoming steadily more industrialized. In general, the natives feel that this is a good thing, provided the industrial concentrations are not too heavy. They do not relish the idea of turning any part of the commonwealth into a vast complex of factories, with blast furnaces belching, soot cascading down and mephitic odors permeating the atmosphere. Fortunately, the industries that are concentrating increasingly in Virginia tend to be of a high type, such as electronics plants and other facilities having to do with the national space program. Generally speaking, the factories are modern and the wages good.

Virginia is making substantial progress as an industrial state. Its major industries include tobacco manufacture, electrical equipment and electronics, paper and paper products, chemicals and chemical products, textiles, furniture, and shipbuilding. The last-named centers in the Newport News Shipbuilding and Dry Dock Company, one of the great shipbuilding companies on the globe, situated on Hampton Roads, one of the world's finest natural harbors.

Among the Old Dominion's principal assets in the industrial sphere is the Federal Government's National Aeronautics and Space Administration's center near Langley Field. This huge $150,000,000 installation, with a $13,000,000 radiation laboratory under construction, has many hundreds of engineers and scientists on its rolls, and thousands of additional technical and support personnel. Graduate programs have been arranged in cooperation with the University of Virginia, Virginia Polytechnic Institute and the College of William and Mary.

Virginia's per capita income is easily the largest in the Southeast, with the exception of Florida's, and these two states are virtually tied. Virginia's per capita figure more than quintupled between 1929 and 1965 (from $435 to $2,419), a substantially better ratio of increase

YEARLINGS ON BROOKMEADE FARMS, PIEDMONT COUNTRY

than that for the country as a whole, which nearly quadrupled during the same period ($703 to $2,746).

One of the foremost industries of Virginia is the tourist industry. Few, if any, states can present the variety of natural and historic attractions for visitors that are to be found in the Old Dominion. The commonwealth was heavily fought over in both the American Revolution and the Civil War; it has produced more Presidents of the United States (eight) and more great generals than any other state, and it boasts some of the most beautiful scenic drives and vistas anywhere.

Many Northerners and Westerners, attracted by the charm and traditions of Virginia, have settled in the state. This has occurred frequently in the horse-raising and fox hunting regions—such as Fauquier and Loudoun Counties on the Northern fringes—and in Albemarle in the Central Piedmont. Various others from

beyond Virginia's boundaries have acquired homes along the beautiful tidal rivers—the Potomac, the Rappahannock, the York and the James. Many a retired capitalist has bought one of the original colonial homes or has built a capacious mansion, from whose veranda he surveys his pastures and stables, or his boat anchorage and duck marshes, his fingers clasping the frosted silver of a julep cup.

Virginians are normally hospitable toward these outlanders who come to settle among them. Some of the more conservative of the natives look down their noses at anyone who seems not to be equipped with a large and stately family tree, but generally speaking there is an absence of provincialism.

However, it is not altogether feasible to generalize concerning Virginians, since there are several subdivisions of the state, and persons in one section some-

LOBLOLLY PINE ON VIRGINIA'S EASTERN SHORE

ORANGE HUNT, THE PLAINS, FAUQUIER COUNTY

times have different reactions, customs and modes of speech from those in another. The principal line of cleavage is between the Easterners and the Westerners —a cleavage that is historic and goes back to the earliest times. The soft accents of Tidewater, where the great pre-Revolutionary mansions line the rivers, contrast with the rather nasal drawl of the mountainous Southwest.

The early settlers of Tidewater included a good many large slave-owners, and were predominantly English, whereas the sturdy frontiersmen who pushed out into the wilderness and settled the back country were mostly Scotch-Irish. The lowlands were, and are, predominantly Democratic, whereas in the highlands Republicans have long been numerous. The picturesque Shenandoah Valley, which the Indians called "The Daughter of the Stars", also harbors many Republicans. Its population includes a large element of Scotch-Irish and Germans, to say nothing of a smattering of Dunkards, or members of the Church of the Brethren, and Amish. The latter wear beards and broad-brimmed black hats, while some of the former still garb themselves similarly and wash one another's feet ceremonially at periodic intervals.

The burnished streams of the Shenandoah Valley run through cavernous limestone country, their limpid and sparkling waters rippling over the stones. Similarly, in the mountainous Southwest the brooks and rivers rush importunately over rocky beds, as trout leap from the pools. But in Piedmont, Southside and Tidewater the sluggish rivers are often muddy, as they roll along under the warm sun, their broad surfaces scarcely ruffled by the catfish and carp underneath.

Historic Virginia is to be found in large measure east of the thriving city of Roanoke, with the greatest concentration in Tidewater, although the Southwest offers distinctly more in the way of storied shrines than many realize. Scenic Virginia is not confined to any single section, and many Eastern Virginians are not aware of the spectacular beauty of the region beyond Roanoke, since great numbers have never been there. After all, it is some 425 miles, as the jet flies, from the dunes of Cape Henry, lashed by Atlantic storms, to Cumberland Gap, on the Kentucky-Virginia line, through which Daniel Boone trekked as he moved westward to hack from the wilderness the settlements beyond the Alleghenies.

CHESAPEAKE BAY LOG CANOES, POPLAR COVE

One of the principal reasons why the brilliant collection of Virginia scenes in this volume from the practiced hand of Aubrey Bodine is so noteworthy, is the emphasis it places on Southwest Virginia—an area often neglected in the past.

For example, most Tidewater Virginians have never seen the state's highest peak, Mount Rogers (5,719 feet) and nearby White Top, only a few feet lower, both near Chilhowie. From White Top one can look down upon the spot where Tennessee, North Carolina and Virginia meet. White Top, before World War II, was famous for its annual music festival, at which mountain fiddlers played tunes handed down from Elizabethan times, and gnarled men from the coves sang ballads which Marlowe and Shakespeare knew.

On the very edge of the Southwest is the Blue Ridge Parkway, a continuation of the Skyline Drive atop the Blue Ridge. It begins at a point between Charlottesville and Waynesboro and continues along the crest of the mountains past Roanoke and down through Floyd and Carroll Counties into North Carolina, to form one of the most beautiful drives on the globe.

The Southwest is the birthplace and home of one of the most significant cultural advances made in Virginia in recent times—the Barter Theatre at Abingdon. Founded at the bottom of the great depression by an extraordinary personality, Robert Porterfield, who devised a novel plan for accepting beans, jam or gladioli offered by impoverished customers in return for theater tickets, it became the first State Theatre in this country.

Barter is also the oldest professional theatre under the same management in the United States, and "Bob" Porterfield has produced more plays than any living American. His troupe is the only one in the U.S. to be invited to present "Hamlet" on its original site—Elsinore Castle in Denmark. It did so some years ago, to great applause. Many famous actors got their training at Barter, including two motion picture Oscar winners, Ernest Borgnine and Gregory Peck. The organization has brought live theatre for the first time to dozens of rural Virginia communities.

"Bob" Porterfield, the dynamo who sparked all this, was born on a beautiful old estate, "Twin Oaks", near Glade Spring in the Abingdon area. Gorgeous oak trees which have stood there since before Columbus, give the place its name, and on the walls of the living room hang the original patents. Eight successive generations of Porterfields have dwelt on that land.

Not many Tidewater families can match this record. Nor can they match the well nigh baronial style in which a few of the Southwestern cattle raisers live. Notable among these are the Stuart family of Russell County. William Alexander Stuart Jr. presides over 25,000 acres. High mountains rise from the blue grass of this vast estate, over which thousands of sheep and cattle roam. Houses and medical care are provided for the scores of families which have lived on the tract for generations, and there is mutual esteem between the tenants and the owner. The U.S. post office of Rosedale on the estate testifies to the magnitude of the operation.

The Southwest cannot compete, however, with other areas of the state in certain fields. Take the city of Williamsburg and nearby Jamestown and Yorktown, both within a fourteen-mile radius of it. Nowhere else is there a comparably historic segment of American soil. At Jamestown, the first permanent English settlement in America was founded thirteen years before Plymouth Rock. Williamsburg was the colonial capital for over three-quarters of a century, and its streets were trod by nearly all the great Virginians of the colonial and

OAK GROVE MENNONITE CHURCHYARD, DAYTON

SUMMER SUNRISE ON AN ATLANTIC BEACH

revolutionary eras. The city has been marvelously restored, along with the Christopher Wren Building at the College of William and Mary, by the late John D. Rockefeller Jr. And, of course, it was at Yorktown that Cornwallis surrendered to Washington, as the band played "The World Turned Upside Down." Some of the epochal events of the seventeenth and eighteenth centuries in Virginia are presented movingly and dramatically each summer in the open air theatre at Williamsburg in Paul Green's drama, "The Common Glory."

But if this small sector of the lower Peninsula between the James and the York is unique, the onetime capital at the falls of the James likewise beckons to the visitor. Richmond is a thriving manufacturing center, but it is also saturated with history, and haunted by the shades of Patrick Henry and John Marshall, Edgar Allan Poe and Jefferson Davis. In the capitol designed by Thomas Jefferson after the Maison Carreé at Nîmes, Aaron Burr was tried for treason, Robert E. Lee received his sword as commander of the Virginia forces in the Civil War, and the body of "Stonewall" Jackson lay in state after he was mortally wounded at Chancellorsville.

Richmond has the undeserved reputation of being a center of ancestor worship second only to the Chinese cities of the pre-Communist era. Will Rogers provoked hearty guffaws when he said some decades ago: "The Prince of Wales was born in Richmond—Richmond, England, of course. He didn't have enough ancestors to be born in Richmond, Virginia."

Will may not have known that the New York Social Register once had a Richmond edition, but it was abandoned because so little interest was shown in it by Richmonders. The fact is that the city's supposed ancestor worship is vastly exaggerated.

In the field of race relations, Richmond has one of the best records in the South. An aggressively integrationist Washington newspaper published a highly complimentary article in 1962 setting forth the manner in which Richmond had pioneered and Negro citizens had been accepted in Richmond's schools, railroad and bus terminals, hotels, restaurants, libraries and so on, before such concessions were made in many Southern cities. Most of these concessions were made in Richmond with great reluctance, it must be admitted, but some were granted without legal compulsion.

The Virginia Museum of Fine Arts at Richmond, the first State Art Museum to be established in the United States, is the foremost art museum in any city of its size in this country, and one of the best on the continent, with collections valued at $20,000,000. Its topflight offerings in music, drama and the dance give this institution a particularly broad cultural spectrum. Its artmobiles and its numerous chapters or affiliates throughout Virginia provide an exceptional statewide impact. Under the imaginative direction of Leslie Cheek Jr. it has attracted international attention.

Richmond is a great medical center, thanks to the Medical College of Virginia and the city's long tradition of skill and research in the healing arts. It is also an educational center. Like the Medical College, the University of Richmond (Baptist) and Union Theological Seminary (Presbyterian) are both well over a century old.

In Richmond too, is the Virginia Historical Society, with a huge and valuable collection of materials, housed in a new and modern headquarters built as an annex to Battle Abbey, which the Society owns. And there is the Valentine Museum, with a priceless collection bearing on the history of the city, situated in the beautiful old Wickham mansion.

The City of Norfolk is enjoying a forward surge that has enlisted much admiration. Now the largest city in the state in population—until Richmond manages to annex additional territory—it has made extraordinary progress in both material and cultural realms.

Norfolk's excellent symphony orchestra is older than Richmond's equally fine musical organization, and the Norfolk Symphony generously permitted its able conductor, Edgar Schenkman, to divide his time between the two cities. Norfolk's annual International Azalea Festival also is winning great acclaim.

Norfolk, furthermore, is the site of the greatest naval base on earth and the world's largest coal pier, and the

POWELL VALLEY MINER

city is now linked with the Eastern Shore by the unique 17-mile-long Chesapeake Bay Bridge-Tunnel. It is enjoying a boom which seems destined to reach even greater heights.

The Eastern Shore of Virginia, comprising the two ancient counties of Accomack and Northampton, with history and traditions going back more than three centuries, probably will be transformed in a decade or two, when the full effect of the bridge-tunnel is felt.

However, this picturesque peninsula between the ocean and the bay, may be expected to change slowly. Its fishermen, oystermen, clam-diggers, lumbermen, poultrymen and farmers are pursuing the even tenor of their way, not greatly affected by the onrushing automotive age—or even the space age. This last is brought into direct contact with them by virtue of the presence on the Shore of the Wallops Island Station operated by the National Aeronautics and Space Administration.

To sum up, Virginia is a composite of many elements, many ingredients. The impact of the state's intellectual milieu, its unhurried way of life on the mind of the visitor is seen in the declaration of the late Count Hermann Keyserling, who wrote:

"The only real cultural atmosphere one finds today in America is that of Virginia. The cultured men who were born in its field of force are responsible for most that is of cultural value in America. But how different Virginia is from all other states! Its culture is a particular one; it is not only a matter of age but of kind as well."

Winston Churchill wrote, following a visit to Virginia in the 1930's:

"It takes only a few hours by train or motor to go from Washington to Richmond, but we breathe a different air. It is another country . . . . Mellow light plays around long-beleaguered, valiantly defended, world-famous Virginia. The hum of Chicago, the rattle of Wall Street, the roar of New York, the even tranquil prosperity of California, all are absent. We have entered the domain of history. We march with Lee and Jackson, with Stuart and Longstreet, and with early autumn through woods lonely in their leafy splendors, old gold and fading crimson."

Finally, there are the words of still another European, Dr. Ernst Beutler, director of the Goethe Museum at Frankfurt, Germany, who visited the United States about a third of a century ago, and wrote in a review on his return:

"Of all the states, none appealed to me so much, from the point of view of scenery, as well as that of habit of life and thought, as Virginia. Of the university towns, those which fascinated me most were the ones which combine an atmosphere of learning with a natural setting: Princeton, Ithaca, Madison; Bloomington, Ann Arbor, and, most beautiful of all, Charlottesville."

The foregoing tributes are striking, and they come from men with divergent personalities and philosophies. The accuracy of their favorable judgments is borne out in various ways.

In literature and art, for example, Virginia is setting a high standard. Ellen Glasgow, James Branch Cabell and Douglas Southall Freeman are gone, but there are others to hold high the torch.

A partial list would include Clifford Dowdey, recognized as a preeminent Civil War historian and a novelist as well; John Dos Passos, who has a home on the Northern Neck where he spent much of his boyhood, and is writing superior history and fiction; William Styron, Prix de Rome winner and one of the most accomplished novelists writing today; David J. Mays, whose great biography of Edmund Pendleton won the Pulitzer Prize; Mary Wells Ashworth, co-author of the seventh and last volume of Freeman's "George Washington," which also was awarded the Pulitzer Prize; Lenoir Chambers, author of the definitive life of "Stonewall" Jackson; Louis D. Rubin Jr., known both as critic and novelist; Rebecca Yancey Williams, whose delightful "The Vanishing Virginian" helped the country forget its cares during World War II; Virgil Carrington Jones and James I. Robertson Jr., whose works on the Civil War have been valuable; Murrell Edmunds, novelist, poet and playwright; James Jackson Kilpatrick, talented writer in the field of contemporary affairs, Robert Douthat Meade, able biographer; and at least three nationally-known poets: Carleton Drewry, Nancy Byrd Turner and Leigh Hanes.

Among artists of national reputation there are several Virginians. A partial list would include the painters Robert Gwathmey, Julien Binford, Bernard Perlin and Charles Smith—some of whom are not working in Virginia.

The passing of John Powell deprived Virginia of the most eminent musician and composer the state has produced, but there remain such figures as Marjorie Mitchell, pianist; Dorothy Maynor, singer, Camilla Williams, singer.

The foregoing names evidence the progress being made by Virginia on certain specific fronts. The state is advancing similarly on others. A third of a century ago one sometimes heard the phrase "Poor old Virginia." Not so today. The most venerable state in the Union is showing signs of youthful *élan*. It is following the advice of Thomas Jefferson not to "use its traditions for a rocking chair."

Virginia is on the way.

And one of the best evidences of this is seen in the stunning collection of photographs published herewith from the masterful hand of A. Aubrey Bodine. He has portrayed Virginia, both old and new, with a balance, range, artistry and charm which in my opinion has never been equalled in any portfolio of views of the Old Dominion.

JAMESTOWN SHIPS . . . Full-scale reproductions of the three ships, *Susan Constant, Godspeed,* and *Discovery,* that brought the English visitors to Jamestown in 1607 ride in the basin of Jamestown Festival Park. The voyage from England took several months. The park was built by the Commonwealth of Virginia in 1957.

Tidewater

IN SOME respects the above photograph of the three ships at Jamestown and that of the astronauts on Page 33 are the most unusual ones in the book. Both were a matter of luck; the former with weather, the latter of getting the right four men out of a group of seven.

When I photograph water scenes I always try to arrive before daylight to take advantage of the earliest possible light and whatever atmospheric conditions are available. On this particular day I was set up and ready to shoot as soon as the sun began to rise. What bothered me most of all was the background. I knew that behind the ships were an ugly wharf, parked automobiles and a moored ferry boat. But just as the sun started its climb, swirling mists moved across the James behind the ships,

blotting out the ugly objects and providing a dramatic background for my subject. Hollywood couldn't have planned it better with a scenic effects crew. I think the mist gives an old world feeling to the picture.

In August, 1959 *The Sun* sent me to Langley Field to photograph the original seven astronauts who were undergoing special training at the NASA installation there. This was almost two years before the first shoot. Only four were available that day. I forgot about the picture until we began work on this book. When I dug out the negative I realized that, by chance, the four in my photograph were America's first space men. When I made the picture I felt that Grissom would be the first one up. I was wrong. He was the second.   A. A. B.

TERCENTENARY MONUMENT . . . The 103-foot granite
shaft was erected in 1907 to commemorate the 300th
anniversary of the settlement. The principal area of the
town of Jamestown was along the James River on both
sides of the present monument. Behind this is the visitor
center which has an extensive series of exhibits. Included
are the earrings of Pocahontas.

JAMESTOWN ISLAND . . . This historic spot is a flat oval of marsh and woodland three miles long. At the time of the landing Jamestown was a peninsula, not an island. Erosion has taken about 25 acres of the western section of the townsite. The lower end of the island offers an excellent view of the James River.

JAMES FORT . . . One of the features of Festival Park is James Fort, built to show what life was like in the early days of Jamestown. Costumed guides show visitors the mud-and-thatch houses and ramparts of the fort. Nearby is Chief Powhatan's Lodge. Queen Elizabeth came to America in 1957 for the Jamestown Festival.

25

WILLIAMSBURG . . . The broad public way of historic Williamsburg is Duke of Gloucester Street which has been called "the most historic avenue in all America." It is a mile in length, with the Capitol at one end, the College of William and Mary at the other. At the left above is Chowning's Tavern, where meals are served; next to it is the Red Lion. Three stores are shown in the lower picture. The center building has three sugar loaves hanging from iron trappings, a traditional sign of Colonial grocers.

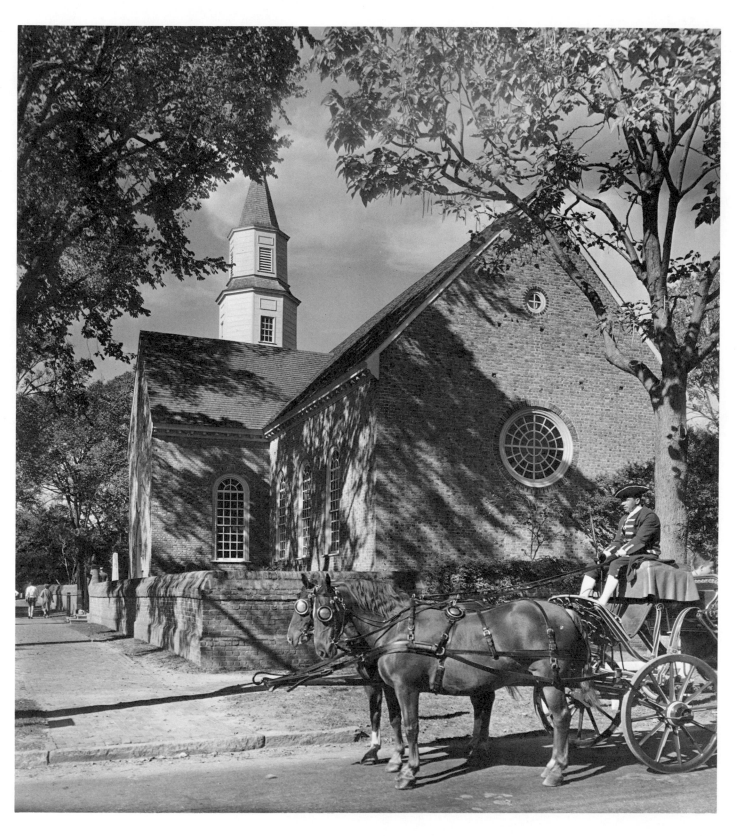

BRUTON PARISH CHURCH . . . One of America's oldest
Episcopal churches, it has been in continuous use since it
was built in 1715 as a court church for the colony. Here
hangs Virginia's "liberty bell" which rang out the news
of the Declaration of Independence and surrender of
Cornwallis. It was the rector of this parish, the late Rev.
Dr. W.A.R. Goodwin who conceived the restoration of
Williamsburg and interested John D. Rockefeller Jr.

RALEIGH TAVERN . . . This was one of the most famous taverns of colonial times. Washington, Jefferson, Patrick Henry, Lafayette dined here. The Raleigh was a center of social activity and balls were held in its Apollo Room. Land, slaves and goods were sold before its door. It was named in honor of Sir Walter Raleigh.

WREN BUILDING . . . The Sir Christopher Wren building of the College of William and Mary, below, is oldest academic building in use in the U.S. There is evidence that it was designed by the famous architect. Started in 1695, it was first building erected on the campus, and is oldest of the restored public buildings in Williamsburg.

GOVERNOR'S PALACE . . . One of the most elegant mansions in colonial America, the Palace was the official residence of seven royal governors, and later the executive mansion for the commonwealth's first two governors, Patrick Henry and Thomas Jefferson. The beautiful building has been reconstructed on its old foundations. The formal gardens are considered among the handsomest in America and include a spectacular English maze.

WINDMILL . . . . This is a post-type windmill with the superstructure revolving on top of a huge post. In a high wind the miller had to turn mariner and furl his canvas sails which were lashed to lattice frames of the four arms. Robertson's Windmill is an operating Craft Shop open to the public, offering "the finest meal ground in Williamsburg." The original had no fixed foundation and so could be moved to a new location.

NAVY YARD . . . The Norfolk Naval Shipyard at Portsmouth is the oldest naval shipyard in the U.S. It was established in 1767 under a British flag. It has felt the impact of nine wars, in which it was burned three times. The yard is built on 811 acres, has 424 buildings, two ways, and seven dry docks capable of handling world's largest ships. The 350-ton crane is a landmark of Elizabeth River area.

GRAIN ELEVATOR . . . This Norfolk grain elevator has a storage capacity of 3,300,000 bushels. The ports of Norfolk, Newport News, Portsmouth and Chesapeake (a consolidation of South Norfolk and Norfolk County) comprise the Greater Hampton Roads, one of the world's greatest natural harbors.

CAR FLOAT . . . Railroad car floats operate on regular schedules across Hampton Roads. Two railroads, the Norfolk and Western and Chesapeake & Ohio, have their principal terminals at Hampton Roads, which has 30 miles of developed waterfront and 25 general cargo piers or wharves.

RECORD BREAKER . . . The *United States* is the largest liner ever built in America. Overall length is 990 feet. She carries 2,000 passengers and a crew of 1,000. The ship was built by the Newport News Shipbuilding and Drydock Company. Picture was made in 1954 when ship returned to Norfolk for overhaul.

LARGEST, FASTEST . . . The $25,000,000 coal pier of the Norfolk & Western Railway at Norfolk is the largest and fastest coal-loading dock in the world. The pier, completed in 1963, can berth four of the largest colliers and has a top loading speed of 20,000 tons an hour. These yards will hold 11,520 coal hopper cars.

MYERS HOUSE . . . The above house was built in 1791 by Moses Myers, merchant and shipowner. It is considered the most interesting example of a late Georgian residence in Norfolk. The house was occupied continuously by members of Myers family until 1931, when it was opened as a museum.

ADAM THOROUGHGOOD . . . Adam Thoroughgood came to America in 1621 as an indentured servant. Before he died at age 35 he was member of the House of Burgesses and owner of some 7,000 acres in Princess Anne County. House, near Norfolk, was built between 1646 and 1660 and is said to be oldest brick house in Virginia.

ASTRONAUTS AND SACLANT . . . The seven astronauts received some of their early training with NASA at Langley Field. These four, photographed on August 3, 1959—nearly two years before the first flight—were the first Americans into space. Left to right: John H. Glenn, Jr. (third up and first into orbit), Virgil I. Grissom (second up), Alan B. Shephard, Jr. (the first), and Malcolm Scott Carpenter (fourth). At the right is a view of Headquarters of the Supreme Allied Command, Atlantic, a part of NATO, which calls itself the world's first international ocean command. Flags of the fifteen NATO members fly at SACLANT'S headquarters.

MacArthur Museum . . . In 1963 Norfolk's old courthouse became the Gen. Douglas MacArthur Museum. It contains his correspondence, war plans and communiques, decorations, battle trophies and gifts. The general's World War II hallmarks, the special hat, dark glasses and corncob pipe, are on display. MacArthur wanted the museum in Norfolk because his mother, Mary Pinckney Hardy, was born, grew up and married there. MacArthur is buried in the museum.

Fort Monroe . . . Jefferson Davis, president of the Confederacy, was held a political prisoner in a casemate of these granite walls from 1865 to 1867. The fort, which stands on Old Point Comfort, was started in 1819. It controlled the channel from Chesapeake Bay to Hampton Roads.

MARINERS MUSEUM . . . This museum is devoted to the culture of the sea and its tributaries . . . Its conquest by man and its influence on civilization. Exhibits include over 80 carved figureheads, ship models, whaling and fishing equipment, sailors' handiwork and tools. The library contains some 40,000 books and pamphlets and 70,000 photographs. The Museum, in Newport News, stands in a park and game sanctuary of 880 acres on the James River, near Hampton Roads, scene of the battle of the *Monitor* and *Virginia* (once the *Merrimac*).

MYSTERY SHIP . . . This photograph of the schooner *Doris Hamlin* was made in 1939 in Hampton Roads. The next year the four-master, loaded with coal and carrying a crew of ten, disappeared while bound for the Canary Islands. No trace of the ship has ever been found. The wooden ship was built in Delaware in 1919. During its eventful life it carried coal to Martinique, logwood from Haiti, college students to Bermuda. It had a displacement of 1,500 tons. The masts towered 117 feet above deck.

N. S. ENTERPRISE . . . The world's largest warship and only nuclear-powered aircraft carrier, the *N. S. Enterprise* dwarfs several tugboats as it moves up the James River. The 85,000-ton vessel was built at Newport News shipyard at a cost exceeding $400,000,000. Its electric generating capacity could serve a city of 2,000,000, and from keel to mast the carrier rises 23 stories. Water-cooled nuclear reactors give it the capability of steaming 5 years without refueling. It is 1,040 feet long and 252 feet wide. The *Enterprise* was employed in Vietnam where planes were launched against the enemy from the 4.5 acre flight deck. On-board facilities include a hospital.

NORFOLK'S CIVIC CENTER . . . The Public Safety Building, left, the 16-story City Hall, center, and the Courts Buildings, right, on St. Paul's Boulevard, are the bright face of a revitalized Norfolk, which has a population of approximately 321,000 and is the largest city in Virginia. The buildings all were erected within the last five years in a renewal area once made up largely of slums on what was old east Main Street. The Civic Center overlooks the Elizabeth River, and adjacent to the center is the tallest building in Virginia. It is the 23-story Virginia National Bank Building, which was completed in 1967 in this city of dynamic growth.

BRIDGE-TUNNEL . . . The 17.5-mile bridge-tunnel across the mouth of the Chesapeake Bay connects the Eastern Shore with the Virginia mainland near Norfolk. The $200,000,000 facility eliminates the last water barrier on the Ocean Highway between New York and Jacksonville, Fla. The two-lane project consists of about thirteen miles of trestle, one-and-a-half miles of earth-fill causeway, two bridges totalling a mile in length, and two tunnels each more than a mile long that pass under the Thimble Shoals and Baltimore ship channels. The man-made island in the foreground is one of four anchoring the tunnels; each is eight acres. A ship is passing over one of the tunnels. A trip across the bridge-tunnel takes about 25 minutes. Below, one of the seven ferries the bridge-tunnel replaces.

BAY BOAT AND FERRY . . . The *City of Richmond,* above, headed for Norfolk. It was one of the ships operated by the Baltimore Steam Packet Company, more familiarly known as the Old Bay Line, between Norfolk and Washington and Norfolk and Baltimore. The company was founded in 1840; service was discontinued in 1962. It was the oldest overnight steamboat line in the country. Below, one of the two state-owned car ferries that cross the James River. This one is leaving Scotland Wharf for Jamestown. Trip takes twenty minutes.

BAY SAILING . . . The Chesapeake Bay is one of the best sailing areas in the United States. Along its shores are hundreds of yacht clubs, boat clubs and marinas. Bay waters are used just about the year round by a variety of craft, ranging from ancient log canoes to sleek ocean-racing yachts.

LANDMARKS . . . Cape Henry has two lighthouses. The one in the background, built in 1791, was the first one erected by the U.S. Government. It is now under the jurisdiction of the Association for the Preservation of Virginia Antiquities. Its replacement was built in 1881. Its light is visible nineteen miles at sea.

39

INLAND WATERWAY . . . One of the links in the Inland Waterway is the Albemarle and Chesapeake sector which connects the Chesapeake area with the Carolina Sounds. This is Great Bridge, western terminus of the 11-mile canal which was built to eliminate outside passage around Cape Hatteras for smaller vessels.

LAKE DRUMMOND . . . The heart of the Dismal Swamp and its most striking feature is Lake Drummond. Giant cypress rise from the water, and along the shore is a dense forest. The lake is the highest point of the Swamp, 22.2 feet above the sea, and the rest of the Swamp slopes away from it. It can best be imagined as the cavity at the top of an inverted saucer. The Dismal Swamp, which extends into North Carolina, is as large as the State of Rhode Island.

OCEAN TRAWLERS . . . Hampton is home port for a fleet of trawlers that work along the Atlantic Coast, dragging nets over the ocean floor in search of fish. Most favored grounds are off North Carolina. The biggest catch is porgy, followed by sea bass and flounder. Deep-sea fishing from Hampton started in the 1930's. The catch has grown to about 20,000,000 pounds a year and accounts for about 90 per cent of the food fish landed at Hampton. A trawler generally carries a crew of five and stays out for days. There are about 50 trawlers in the fleet; many operate the year round. Some fish during the summer from northern ports.

ST. JOHN'S CHURCH . . . The walls of this Hampton church belong to the original structure which was built in 1728. The church was ransacked during War of 1812, restored in 1827-28 and again in 1869 after a fire. Many of town's founders are buried in the churchyard.

SMITH'S FORT PLANTATION . . . Thomas Warren built this house about 1652 on plantation of John Rolfe, father of American tobacco industry. It is often called the "Rolfe House." Nearby are the remains of Smith's Fort, built by Capt. John Smith in 1609 as protection against the Indians and Spanish. It was later used as a public landing.

HAMPTON ROADS . . . Some 6,000 ships sail from Hampton Roads every year to nearly 350 ports in the free world. Nearly 50,000,000 tons of water-borne commerce move through Hampton Roads each year and the port has led all North Atlantic ports in export tonnage for years. About 200,000 tons of tobacco are exported annually.

ST. LUKE'S . . . Once called the Old Brick Church, this mellow red brick building, near Smithfield, was started, according to local tradition, in 1632 and if so, relates closely to the Tower Church at Jamestown. St. Luke's historians claim this is oldest existing church of English foundation in the United States.

SMITHFIELD HAMS . . . According to Virginia law, only the four packing companies in Smithfield are permitted to produce the famed Smithfield ham. To achieve the distinctive flavor, peanut-fed hogs are used. Hams hang over hickory log fires for weeks. Some 300,000 are shipped each year throughout America and abroad.

SUN AND SURF . . . Virginia Beach, which stretches for eight miles, is the state's seaside playground from May through October. Average temperature is 68.8. The resort has all types of fishing and year-round golf. Summer population exceeds 50,000.

SURF CASTING . . . Fishermen with long rods stand in the surf of the Atlantic Ocean as they fish for red drum, which put up a good fight in the surf and shoals. Virginia's ocean front is about 110 miles long, most of it on the Eastern Shore.

OYSTER TONGERS . . . Tongers work the oyster seed beds of the James River, said to be the finest such beds in the world. The spat, the newly set oyster, grows better here than any other place, but, for unknown reasons, the oysters never attain much size. So they are sold as seed and transplanted in other waters where they grow large and fat. Virginia is the world's largest oyster producer. Above, James River tongers anchored at Deep Creek.

PEANUTS . . . Peanut vines, left, are shocked for curing after October harvest. Single vine may have from 25 to 50 nuts. The peanut, of course, is not a nut but a vegetable and grows like a potato. Virginia is a great peanut-producing state and most of the crop is grown in tidewater. Center for the industry is Suffolk, Virginia.

SNAPPER TRAPPER . . . A Virginia waterman lowers a trap for snapping turtles between two cypress trees in the Chickahominy River. He sells to a packer in Toano, who for years, has been shipping more than 100,000 pounds of snappers, 25,000 pounds of eels and 200,000 pounds of catfish annually. Some catfish weigh 25 pounds.

MOTHBALL FLEET . . . Row after row of ships, 350 in all, are anchored in the James River as part of the U.S. Merchant Marine Reserve Fleet. They include 150 World War II Liberties, passenger ships and a number of C class freighters. During the early 1950's the Government used 50 Liberties on an emergency basis to store 8,000,000 bushels of surplus grain.

WESTOVER . . . Probably the most famous of the James River plantation houses, this fine example of Georgian architecture was built in 1730 by William Byrd II who collected one of the best libraries of his day. The interior is noted for beautiful proportion of its rooms, detail of ceiling and cornice, and unusual black mantelpiece.

MERCHANT'S HOPE CHURCH . . . This is one of Virginia's oldest churches, built about 1657. The unusual name derived from a barque, *The Merchant's Hope,* which plied between England and Virginia. Some claim that the brickwork "is the most beautiful in America." The church is five miles east of Hopewell in Prince George County.

CARTER'S GROVE . . . The mansion, above, is on the James River. It was built between June and September of 1751 at a cost of 500 pounds. Extensively altered in 1927, it is now entrusted to Colonial Williamsburg, and the estate once owned by "King" Carter is open to the public daily, March through November.

SHIRLEY . . . Home of the Carter family since the early days of the 18th century. It was visited by Robert E. Lee, whose mother was Anne Hill Carter. The mansion is noted for its superb paneling and carved walnut stair. Four nearby brick buildings form a noted Queen Anne fore-court. They probably were erected before 1750.

BRANDON PLANTATION . . . This ranks as one of the most magnificent of the James River plantations and has beautiful gardens that extend to the river. The land was once owned by John Martin, companion of Capt. John Smith on his first voyage to America. The estate comprises 5,000 acres, mostly in grains and pasture.

BACON'S CASTLE . . . The house below is said to be the only true Jacobean house in America and one of few relics of Bacon's Rebellion which preceded the Revolution by 100 years. Nathaniel Bacon never lived here but it was the last place held by his followers. The house, built about 1655, is noted for its cluster chimneys.

YORKTOWN . . . The ornate Victory Monument commemorates the French alliance and the victory over Lord Cornwallis who surrendered after his British Army was besieged by the troops of Washington and Rochambeau while Count de Grasse, the French admiral, blocked rescue from the sea. The surrender marked the virtual close of the American Revolution and ended six-and-a-half years of war. The victory came 174 years after the founding of the first permanent English settlement at Jamestown.

CUSTOMS HOUSE . . . This building, erected about 1720 and restored in 1929, stands on Main Street in Yorktown, a block from the waterfront. Edward Ambler, collector of revenues, participated in Virginia's "Tea Party" on Nov. 3, 1774 when residents of the town boarded the *Virginia* and dumped two half-chests of tea overboard.

MOORE HOUSE, YORKTOWN . . . Commissioners representing American, French and British forces met here Oct. 18, 1781 to arrange articles of surrender for Cornwallis' army. It was home of Augustine Moore in days of Revolution. Family pieces in the house at time of surrender have recently been located and restored.

NELSON HOUSE . . . The Yorktown mansion is named for its builder, William Nelson, who completed it about 1740. While Cornwallis occupied the house during the siege of 1781, General Thomas Nelson directed a cannonade against his own home and offered a prize to the soldier who hit it. A ball is still in one wall, right.

N.S. SAVANNAH . . . The nation's first atom-powered cargo ship, N.S. *Savannah,* docked at the U.S. Coast Guard Training Center, Yorktown, during a visit to Virginia. The ship, which cost $53,500,000, can cruise for more than three years without refueling. The Yorktown center trains thousands of Coast Guard reservists each year.

SHADOW, VIRGINIA . . . The farmer brought two bushels of clams and four chickens to town in his two-wheel cart to barter for staples. He stands before the post office, trading center and meeting place for Shadow. Virginia has many towns with colorful names: Rescue, Modest Town, Lively, Burnt Chimneys, Bumpass, and Hurt.

HORN HARBOR . . . This busy fishing center lies northeast of Mobjack Bay and is one of the most picturesque sections of tidewater Virginia. The weathered poles are 60 to 70 feet long and cost about $10 apiece. They are known as pound stakes, trap stakes or weir poles, and are pulled out of the water at the end of the season.

TIDE MILL . . . The huge wooden wheel turned one way when the tide flowed into the cove, the other way when it ebbed out. The mill is on Mobjack Bay and is the last one in the Bay country. Its exact age is not known, but records indicate that it ground grain for Washington's army during the siege of Yorktown in 1781.

MERRY POINT FERRY . . . Travelers on Route 644 in the Northern Neck cross the Corotoman River on a cable ferry. It is powered by a boat and guided by an underwater cable. A ferry has been used to cross the river, here a half mile wide, for 125 years. It is now state operated. There is no charge for the crossing.

FLEETS BAY NECK . . . This photograph was a prize winner in the National Press Photographers contest in 1963. The area, near White Stone and Irvington, is a famed oyster, crab and fishing grounds. The small island in the background is edged with some graceful loblolly pine.

SHELL GAME . . . A scow is loaded with oyster shells which will be used to "shell" a soft or muddy bottom as a means of building a foundation on which seed oysters should grow. Planters might dump as many as 20,000 bushels of shells on four acres. They sell for about 15 cents a bushel. The waterman holds 32-foot tongs, some of the longest in the Chesapeake Bay.

CHESAPEAKE WATERMAN . . . He knows the Bay, its weather and where the oysters, crab and fish are to be found. Most of all, he's a rugged individualist who works when he pleases and sits on his porch when he wants to. This man, at the tiller of his boat, is typical of the breed. The photograph won the George Washington gold medal award by the Freedoms Foundation. It was titled, "Free Man."

POUND NETTERS . . . A heavy load of fish is pulled out of the pound net near New Point. A pound net is a large stationary device of poles and netting arranged to form a trap. A net with poles would cost about $3,500. Such nets are generally used from March through November.

CLOSING THE PURSE . . . Fishermen have made a wide circle around a school of menhaden in the lower Bay and are about to draw a purse string that will close the net. After the net is pulled in, the bunched fish are dipped out. The menhaden season runs from May until November.

NET CHECKERS . . . Watermen unreel their menhaden nets at Reedville to check the nets. A net is about 1,200 feet long, 90 feet wide. Menhaden are also known as alewife, oldwife, bunker, mossbunker, bughead, bugfish, and chebog. They are members of the herring family.

INDIAN FISHERMEN . . . Pamunkey Indians gill net for shad in the Spring on the Pamunkey River. They have an 800-acre Reservation on the river. Nearby West Point was once called Pamunkee or Paumnkey and was the chief village of the Paumnkey of the Powhatan Confederacy.

A.P. HILL . . . Troops march past the reviewing stand at Camp A.P. Hill, a 77,000-acre installation in Caroline County used as a training and maneuver area for regular army units and, during the summer, for 25,000 Army Reservists and National Guardsmen. The 29th Division, which consists of Virginia and Maryland men, often trains here. The post is named in honor of Lieut. Gen. Ambrose Powell Hill, C.S.A. who was killed while defending Petersburg.

INDIAN CHIEF . . . Deerfoot Cook is chief of the Pamunkey Indians. He poses with some of the fat shad he has caught. Fishing provides a main source of income for the dwindling tribe. On the other side of the Pamunkey River is a reservation for the Mattaponi tribe.

ANCESTRAL MANSIONS . . . King Carter built homes in Northern Neck for three of his sons, but the only one in existence is Sabine Hall, top left, built in 1730 for Landon Carter. It has belonged to the Carter family, or its descendants, ever since. The house is of brick; the columns of the Grecian portico are of solid cypress. Mount Airy, bottom left, was built by Col. John Tayloe in 1758 and has always been owned by the Tayloe family. It is a fine example of the house and surroundings of an early Virginia planter of the wealthiest class. The mansion, built of native brown sandstone, resembles a great English baronial house more than a colonial one.

COURTHOUSES . . . King William County Courthouse, above, is a T-shaped building with hip roof, end chimneys and an arched loggia. Also on the court green are the clerk's office, jail and Confederate monument. King William is county seat for King William County which was formed in 1701 from King and Queen County. The courthouse of Essex County, below, is in Tappahannock, on the Rappahannock. It was erected in 1848. The old clerk's office, right, was built before 1750. Later a jail, it is now the public library. Court records tell of a woman indicted for swearing "75 oaths" and of another whipped for wearing Governor Spotswood's clothes.

GLOUCESTER C.H. . . . County seat of Gloucester County is tree-shaded and unhurried. The courthouse—with the portico—was erected in 1766. A tablet in the courtroom characterizes Nathaniel Bacon, leader of the 1676 rebellion, as "soldier, statesman, and saint." On the left is the jail and next to it is the clerk's office.

ABINGDON CHURCH . . . The church sits in a grove of walnut trees, behind a brick wall. Abingdon Parish was formed about 1650. This church, near the foundations of an earlier one, probably was completed in 1755. A communion set presented to the parish in 1703 is still used.

WARE CHURCH . . . The parish goes back to about 1650. The date of this church is uncertain, but it probably was built between 1682 and 1723. The first rector was Rev. Alexander Moray (or Murray) who was with Charles II at the Battle of Worcester in 1652. Both Ware and Abingdon churches are in Gloucester County.

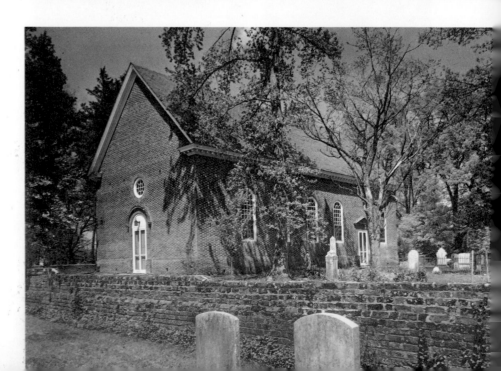

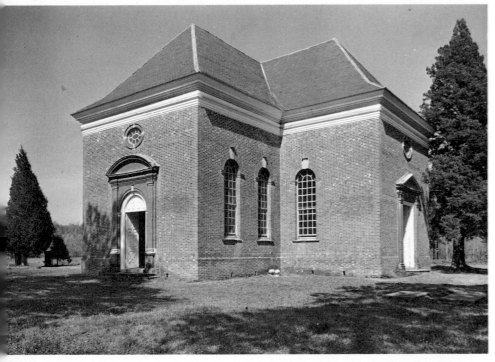

TODDSBURY . . . This brick house, built about 1658, is called "Mother House of Gloucester." The estate was patented by Thomas Todd, an enterprising shipper who amassed vast land holdings in Virginia and Maryland. The house has 15 acres of lawn which slope to the North River.

CHRIST CHURCH . . . This is also called "King Carter's Church" because the entire cost of building was paid by him. It is one of a few colonial churches that has never been altered, and only one in Virginia still having its original furnishings. The church, which stands in Lancaster County near Kilmarnock, was built about 1732.

ONE-ROOM SHRINE . . . Walter Reed, the physician who discovered the cause of yellow fever, was born in this one-room house in 1851, not long after a fire had forced his parents from the Methodist parsonage that was their home. The house, restored as a memorial, is in Gloucester County not far from Ware Church.

LEE'S BIRTHPLACE . . . Robert E. Lee was born in Stratford Hall, opposite, son of Henry Lee, governor of Virginia and Revolutionary War hero. Here also were born Richard Henry Lee and Francis Lightfoot Lee, only brothers to sign the Declaration of Independence. The Westmoreland County mansion, built in the shape of an H, stands on cliffs above the Potomac. The plantation's mill, above, has been rebuilt on the original foundation.

POTOMAC CRUISE . . . Twice a day a 3,000-passenger cruiser makes a trip down the Potomac from Washington to Mount Vernon and a 370-acre amusement park on the opposite shore. The boat passes the Washington National Airport, the Naval Air Station, Bolling Air Force Base, Alexandria and Fort Washington. The picture was made from the fort. At Mount Vernon the boat docks at the original wharf site.

BEACHES . . . Colonial Beach, above, is one of several resort areas on the Potomac. It has a number of hotels and inns and offers a variety of amusements, including a summer festival. The sandy beach stretches for two miles. At Smith Point, left, in Northumberland County, the Chesapeake Bay is some 22 miles broad—its widest point. Gilbert Klingel, naturalist and author of "The Bay," calls Smith Point "one of the most interesting areas in the entire Chesapeake."

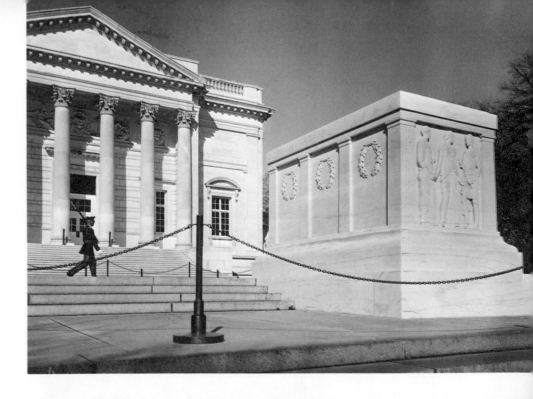

UNKNOWN SOLDIER . . . A sentry, lance-straight, paces in front of the Tomb of the Unknown Soldier in Arlington National Cemetery. The tomb is cut from a single block of marble. Beneath it lies the body of an unknown soldier brought back from France in 1921 and decorated with the Congressional Medal of Honor. The inscription on the tomb reads, "Here rests in honored glory an American Soldier known but to God."

WOODLAWN PLANTATION . . . The rose-red brick house designed in Georgian colonial style was finished in 1805 from plans drawn by Dr. William Thornton on a site selected by George Washington, which was a wedding gift from him to his adopted daughter, Eleanor (Nelly) Parke Custis, who married his nephew, Lawrence Lewis. The 2,000-acre estate was once part of Mount Vernon. It is operated by the National Trust for Historic Preservation.

CUSTIS-LEE MANSION . . . High above the Potomac in Arlington National Cemetery sits a mansion that is famous for its long associations with the families of Custis, Washington and Lee. George Washington Parke Custis, foster son of the First President, began building Arlington House, as it was once known, in 1802. Here Robert E. Lee and Mary Custis, great-granddaughter of Martha Washington, were married and reared a family. Here too Lee wrote his resignation from the U.S. Army to join the cause of Virginia and the South. In 1955 Congress made the mansion a permanent memorial to Robert E. Lee.

GUNSTON HALL . . . Begun by George Mason in 1755, this Fairfax County house near Lorton was finished by William Buckland, the famed builder. The interiors are among the most impressive of the colonial period. The house and the 555-acre estate have been open to the public only since 1952 when they became the property of the Commonwealth of Virginia. Mason was the author of the first constitution of Virginia and of the Virginia "Declaration of Rights" which became the basis of the Federal Bill of Rights. Jefferson called Mason, who died at Gunston, "The wisest man of his generation."

FLAG RAISING . . . The inspiring scene of six tired men raising the flag on Mount Suribachi in 1945 is commemorated by the Marine Corps War Memorial. It honors the men who fought on Iwo Jima in World War II and the Marines who preceded them. The memorial, dedicated in 1954, is said to be the largest cast bronze statue in the world. It borders Arlington National Cemetery and is one of the most visited and photographed shrines in the Washington area.

"THE HIGH SCHOOL" . . . The Episcopal High School in Alexandria was founded in 1839. It probably is the oldest Episcopal boarding school for boys in the U.S. Since its founding antedates the development of any substantial public high school movement in the South it was often referred to as "The High School." The term is still used.

COURTHOUSE AND SHAD RUN . . . Fairfax County Courthouse stands within a stone-walled green in Fairfax. It was built in 1800 when the county seat was moved from Alexandria. On display are the wills of George and Martha Washington. Below right, fishing for spring shad in the Potomac below Washington's Chain Bridge.

CHRIST CHURCH . . . Alexandria's Christ Church was built in 1767-73. The tower and cupola, and probably the balcony, were added in 1818. The family pews of George Washington and Robert E. Lee adjoin. Washington was a vestryman of the parish for a short time in 1765. Lee was confirmed here in 1853.

MEETING HOUSE . . . The old Presbyterian Meeting House in Alexandria, below, was built in 1774 and has, in the words of a guidebook, "a distinction in its very plainness." Tomb of Unknown Soldier of Revolution is in churchyard along with the grave of Dr. James Craik, Washington's surgeon-general, life long physician and friend.

NEW AND THE OLD . . . The Temple of Beth El in Alexandria, top left, was built in 1957 to serve Northern Virginia. Inscribed on the tablets are the Ten Commandments. The congregation was founded in 1859. The first Jews reached Virginia in 1624. Bottom left is the Dr. William Brown house on Fairfax Street in Alexandria. It was built prior to the Revolution on lot once owned by Augustine Washington, brother of George. A hand-hewn stone sink is in the old kitchen. Dr. Brown was one of the first surgeons-general of the Revolutionary Army. He helped arrange the use of Hessian prisoners to pave streets of Alexandria.

POHICK CHURCH . . . This was the parish church of Mount Vernon, Gunston and Woodlawn. Washington helped select the site for the church, completed in 1774. He purchased two pews to help defray building costs and served on the parish vestry for 22 years (1762-1784). He frequently attended services. Pohick was one of the last churches built during the union of church and state.

FALLS CHURCH . . . This Fairfax County church, below, was built in 1767-69 on the site of older churches. During the Revolution it was used as a recruiting station, and as a hospital and later as a stable by Union troops in 1862-64. After the war Congress appropriated $1,300 to restore it.

MASONIC TEMPLE . . . The stone monument occupies the site in Alexandria first proposed for the National Capitol. The full title of the shrine is George Washington Masonic National Memorial Temple. The tower rises in three stages to a stepped pyramid 400 feet high. The cornerstone was laid in 1923. The temple cost $5,000,000 and the money was contributed by more than 3,000,000 Masons.

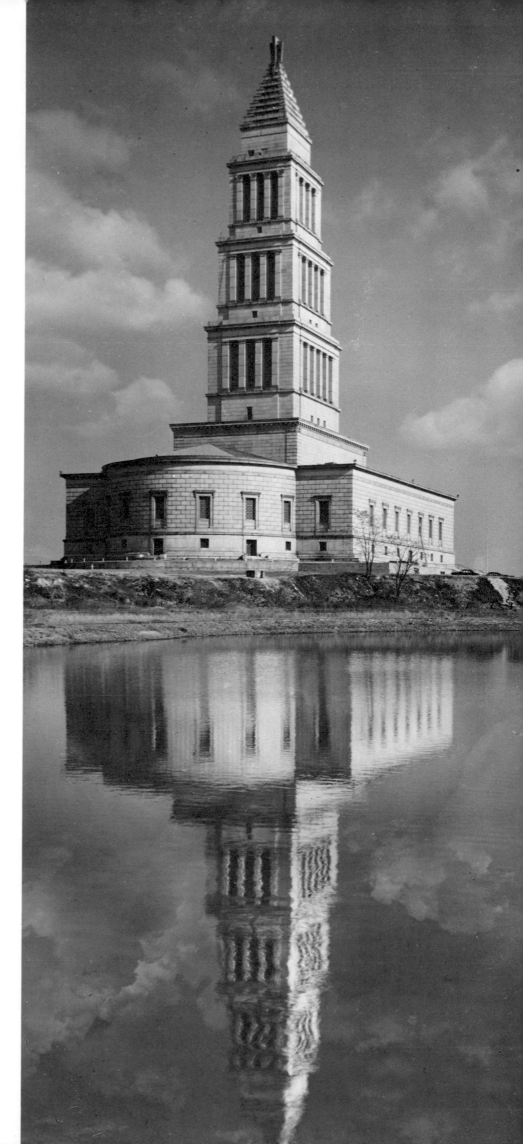

KERR HOUSE . . . The Georgian mansion, top photograph, was built in 1779 on a 1,500-acre tract in Onancock on the Eastern Shore. The drawing room walls were once covered with block-print paper made in Paris. Called one of the handsomest mansions of the area, it is now the home of the Eastern Shore of Virginia Historical Society.

WARWICK . . . Some sources claim that this is the oldest house on Virginia's Eastern Shore. It is said to have been built in 1670. The earliest graves on the Shore are in a nearby burying ground. Partially burned by the British during the Revolution, Warwick has been repaired, restored and added to by its many owners.

SHORE POTATOES . . . Virginia is the leading state in producing early potatoes and 90 per cent of its crop comes from the rich land of the Shore where potatoes are the biggest crop. The annual yield brings about $8,000,000. Harvesting begins in the latter part of June and continues well into July. It is done in the early morning and late afternoon. Potatoes are unearthed by tractor-drawn diggers which scoop them up, shake the dirt away and leave them on top of the ground. Field hands move behind the diggers and gather the potatoes into baskets.

SHORELINES . . . This unusual photograph was made against the sun from a high-flying airplane over a vast marsh on the ocean side of the Shore. The area abounds with wildlife. Virginia has two counties on this side of the Bay, Northampton and Accomack.

POUND NETTERS . . . It takes twelve strong men to draw a pound net heavy with fish. Such nets are generally used in water up to 40 feet deep. Some nets are 1,500 feet long. The stakes mark the boundaries of other nets. The pound net or weir, called "ware" by waterman, is much used in the Chesapeake Bay area.

CLAMMING . . . Ocean clammers range far out into the Atlantic. One of best areas is the "Jack Spot," about 22 miles off shore and a famous marlin grounds. Ocean clams weigh a pound or more. Clamming is also done in the Shore's shallow waters. Above, watermen remove clams from a large float where they are kept for a few days. The dead gull on the post keeps others of its kind from stealing the catch.

CHINCOTEAGUE . . . This famous island is connected with the Shore by a five-mile causeway visible in the top left part of the photograph. The island, which has a population of about 4,000, is a center for both commercial and sports fishing. Chincoteague oysters are nationally famous for their taste and their size.

PONY ROUNDUP . . . Wild ponies from Assateague Island are herded across the 400-foot channel to Chincoteague for the pony penning roundup which climaxes the fireman's carnival every July. The shaggy ponies bring up to $200 at auction. A best-selling children's book and a movie were based on life of a pony named "Misty."

DECOY MAKER . . . A Chincoteague waterman spends his spare time carving ducks and geese. Decoy makers take pride in their coloring, but even more important than color is balance. A decoy must be weighted so that it rides in the water properly. It also must be durable. Decoys are carved from seasoned wood.

SHIPWRECK . . . Two men inspect the shattered hulk of a derelict at Assateague. The island has been searched many times for the treasure of Charles Wilson, a pirate, who buried "in ten iron-bound chests, bars of silver, gold, diamonds and jewels to the sum of £200,000" between three cedar trees near Chincoteague Bay.

OSPREY NEST . . . A student of wild
life goes out on a limb to photograph
an osprey nest. Ospreys, also known
as fish hawks, are common summer
residents of tidewater Virginia and
Maryland. Their bulky nests, generally
constructed of such things as sticks,
splintered boards, sea grass and corn-
stalks, are to be seen on dead trees, pil-
ings, power lines and duck blinds.
They are called birds of prey but their
only prey is fish.

HAMPTON INSTITUTE . . . The school
was founded in 1868 to meet the needs
of former slaves who had found refuge
behind the Union lines on the Virginia
peninsula. The first classroom building
was erected in 1871 with the help of
the American Missionary Association,
the Freedmen's Bureau and Northern
philanthropists. The college today has
a 74-acre waterfront campus with 150
buildings and an enrollment of some
1,600 students. The Institute is in the
city of Hampton. The Huntington
Library is shown.

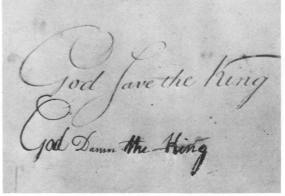

ACCOMAC . . . This small building with the barred windows was once the debtors' prison in Accomac, seat of Accomack County (town and county are spelled differently). It was erected about 1731. Above is part of a page from a court ledger of 1776 in which an unknown but fearless individual recorded his opinion of the King of England during the Revolution. The ledger is in the Accomac courthouse.

ST. GEORGE'S . . . This Accomack County landmark was originally known as Pungoteague church. The parish was formed in 1662. The church, on the site of a frame one that dated to about 1676, was built in 1738. During the War Between the States the church was used by Union troops and left a wreck. One wing was badly damaged by the removal of bricks to erect a cook house for soldiers. The building was rebuilt about 1880. By this time nave and chancel wings had become so ruinous that they were torn down and the bricks used to close openings left in the transept walls. Today it is a plain rectangular building and much of its original charm has disappeared.

OYSTER . . . Not far from the tip of the Shore peninsula, on the ocean side, is a small town which owes its existence to the oyster and consequently it is named Oyster, Va. Three other Eastern Shore villages also are named in honor of the oyster: Bivalve, Oyster-shell and Shelltown.

WALLOPS ISLAND . . . From concrete pads on the beaches at Wallops Island on the Shore, small experimental rockets and missiles roar out over the Atlantic on an average of once a day. A test facility of the National Aeronautics and Space Administration, Wallops Station is a proving ground for ideas and vehicles developed at NASA's Goddard Space Flight Center and other labs. It also provides launching, tracking and telemetering facilities for scientific experiments in space.

OAK GROVE . . . Oak Grove Methodist church, near Keller in Accomack county, has a Sunday school dating from 1785, believed to be the earliest one still in existence in the U.S. The parish started under the name of Burton's Chapel. It is one of the first Methodist congregations on the Shore. The present structure is not too old.

OLDEST RECORDS . . . Eastville has been a county seat since 1680. On the left is the old clerk's office and next to it the old courthouse, which was built in 1731. Both have been restored. In the new courthouse, just out of view on the left, are county records dating back to 1632. They are said to be the oldest such records in any of the original Colonies.

EYRE HALL . . . This rambling frame house near Eastville was the center of the Eyre estate which once extended across the lower Shore. The main section was probably built in the last quarter of the 18th century. Behind the house is a buttery and one of the loveliest box gardens in the county.

DAFFODILS—DUCKS . . . Gloucester and Mathews counties have been growing daffodils commercially for about 35 years. Most of the flowers are shipped to northern markets in March and April. Cash value of the crop is more than $250,000. Right, duck hunters wait for action in one of the thousands of blinds that dot the tidewater area.

HUNGARS CHURCH . . . Built in 1742, this is the third church of that name. It has undergone many architectural changes; the major one was shortening the structure by 20 feet. After the Revolution the building fell into disuse. The organ was dismantled and its pipes melted into sinkers for fish nets. This church is at Bridgetown.

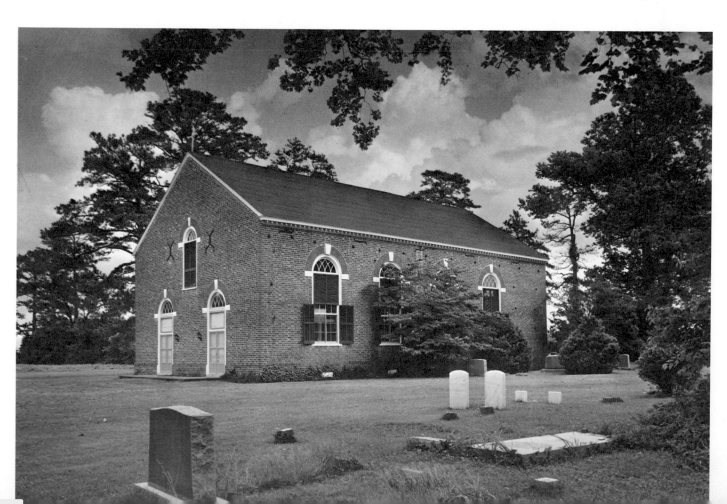

83

FIRING LINE . . . Two hunters raise their guns as a flock of Canada geese wheel by. Mallards, black ducks, pintails and scaup are also shot from these blinds. The scene was photographed off Fox Islands which are just inside the Virginia line. This is one of the most noted gunning areas in the Chesapeake Bay, which has been a famous hunting grounds since the days of the Indian.

TANGIER ISLAND . . . Watermen check the floats where crabs are kept while they peel and become soft crabs. This is Tangier Island, just below the Virginia line in the Bay. Crabbing and oystering are the main sources of income on the four-mile long island which is mostly marsh. The 1,100 inhabitants live along two ridges connected by five bridges. Only bicycles and motor scooters are used.

OYSTER WATCHER . . . On the deck of this house is a woman with a rifle. She has one of the most unusual jobs in tidewater Virginia. She is an oyster watcher. Her job is to keep poachers away from valuable oyster beds which are privately leased. This is in Tom's Cove, near Chincoteague, one of the best oyster grounds in America.

HARD CRABS . . . These crabs have just been unloaded at a Cape Charles dock and are on their way to the steaming shed. Each wire basket holds four barrels of crabs. They are lowered into a vat large enough to hold three baskets. The crabs are steamed for 17 minutes and then sent to the packing house where they are picked.

TERRAPIN . . . A Chincoteague Island waterman checks the diamondback terrapin in his pound. He sells about 4,000 a year to eastern clubs and hotels. The traditional Chesapeake delicacy is today mainly a showcase dish at elaborate dinners. Once sold for $4 apiece, terrapin now bring only about $18 a dozen. Most are caught in marshes with nets.

SHARK FISHING . . . Northampton county fishermen use gill nets to snare sharks in Great Marchipongo inlet. Catch ranges between three and five feet in length. Sharks are sold as a food fish but never called by that name in markets. They are generally known as steakfish or grayfish. Virginia sharks, usually the sand species, have white flaky meat from which fishy flavor and bones are absent.

WAKEFIELD, MOUNT VERNON, MONTICELLO . . . The story-and-a-half house, above, is a reconstruction of Wakefield where George Washington was born on February 22, 1732. It stands in Westmoreland County and is now a national monument on a 400-acre reservation. Between 1754 and 1799 Washington developed Mount Vernon, right above, into one of the finest estates of the period. His land holdings grew from 2,126 to more than 8,000 acres, and the modest nine-room house he inherited was more than doubled in size. Washington once wrote of his home, "No estate in United America is more pleasantly situated than this." Since 1858 Mount Vernon has been owned and maintained by the Mount Vernon Ladies' Association. Monticello, below, was Thomas Jefferson's home from 1770 until his death in 1826. The estate, a few miles from Charlottesville, is one of the most imposing in Virginia, and is also a national shrine.

The Nine Presidents

I HAVE photographed Mount Vernon many times. I usually make the pictures in early spring, before the foliage hides too much of the mansion. In the left foreground of every shot I had what appeared to be a dead tree. Before I made a new picture for this book I suggested to my friend, Charles C. Wall, resident director, that the dead tree be chopped down. He grinned and said, "That's not dead. It's a pecan tree. It's always behind the others." So I returned several weeks later to get the "dead tree" in leaf.

I had trouble locating President Taylor's birthplace because there are two Montebellos in Orange County. (The other is pictured on Page 111.) Incidentally, it's worth a long trip to Montebello just to view the boxwood. This is the largest and grandest I have ever seen.

Some will probably think that I photographed the wrong house at Ash Lawn (Page 90). This is actually the part where Monroe lived. Most photographers shoot the front of the house, which was built much later. The angle I used presented interesting technical problems because I had to shoot directly into the sun.

Oak Hill (Page 90) is a new view of an old house. Just recently workmen removed the unsightly plaster that covered the lovely salmon-colored bricks. The work was done by hand so the bricks would not be damaged.

I had to secure permission to photograph Glen Ora because President Kennedy and his family were still using it as a weekend retreat. The White House arranged a special appointment and I was escorted around the grounds by Secret Service men.   A. A. B.

MONTPELIER . . . This Orange County mansion facing the Blue Ridge Mountains was once the home of James Madison, fourth President of the United States and "Father of the Constitution." Madison retired to Montpelier in 1817 with his beautiful wife Dolly, one of America's most accomplished hostesses. The mansion was suited for the lavish entertainment of the Madisons. Once dinner was served for 90 people. The central portion of Montpelier was built by Madison's father about 1760. The portico was added at the suggestion of Thomas Jefferson. Plans for the garden were made by General Lafayette while visiting the Madisons in 1824.

MONROE'S HOMES . . . Construction of Oak Hill, left, was begun in 1820, during James Monroe's first term as President. Plans for the Loudoun County mansion were drawn by Thomas Jefferson. Here Monroe drafted the message that became famous as the Monroe Doctrine. He built Ash Lawn, below, in Albemarle County to be near his friend Jefferson. It was to have been constructed in two sections, but only the small rear part was finished by him, this in 1798. Ash Lawn was Monroe's home until 1820.

HOME OF THE HARRISONS . . . Berkeley, above, was the
birthplace of a signer of the Declaration of Independence
—Benjamin Harrison—of a president of the United
States—William Henry Harrison—and ancestral home of
another President—Benjamin Harrison. The brick
mansion, which stands on the James River in Charles
City County, was begun in 1726.

GREENWAY . . . John Tyler, tenth president of the United
States, was born March 29, 1790 at Greenway, Charles
City County, below, only a short distance from birthplace
of William Henry Harrison. Tyler was vice president
under Harrison and succeeded to the presidency in 1841
upon the latter's death after only a month in office. Tyler
and his father were both governors of Virginia.

SHERWOOD FOREST . . . After his term as president ended in 1845, John Tyler retired to Sherwood Forest, above, which he purchased in 1842. The colonial house rambles from a central unit through wings and dependencies, all connected. It is about 300 feet long, said to be longest house in Virginia.

MONTEBELLO . . . Zachary Taylor, twelfth President, was born in Orange County, probably at Montebello, on November 24, 1784. The house no longer stands but this building, below, is on the original foundation. Taylor served with distinction in the War with Mexico. He was called "Old Rough and Ready."

WILSON HOUSE . . . Woodrow Wilson, twenty-eighth President, was born here December 28, 1856. His father was pastor of Staunton's First Presbyterian Church and this was the manse of the church. The house was built in 1846 and has been somewhat altered. It is operated by the Woodrow Wilson Memorial Foundation.

GLEN ORA . . . In 1961-62 Mr. and Mrs. John F. Kennedy leased Glen Ora, below, as a weekend retreat from Washington during his first years in the White House. The 450-acre estate, near Middleburg, is in the heart of the Virginia hunt country. Mrs. Kennedy has often ridden with many of the hunts.

CAPITOL . . . Thomas Jefferson was the principal designer of the state capitol in Richmond, above. His inspiration was a Roman temple at Nîmes, France. Here Aaron Burr was tried for treason, Virginia ratified the Articles of Secession and the Confederate Congress met. In the rotunda is Houdon's renowned statue of Washington. The capitol's wings were added in the early 1900's.

BATTLE ABBEY . . . The name on the Ionic portico is Virginia Historical Society, but the building is known as Battle Abbey. It originally was the home of the Confederate Memorial Association which was absorbed by the Historical Society in 1946. Enlarged several times, it contains manuscripts, books, furniture, weapons and murals depicting the four seasons of the Confederacy.

VIRGINIA MUSEUM OF FINE ARTS . . . Opened in 1936, this handsome building is headquarters for the nation's first statewide confederation of arts organizations. The world's first "artmobiles" carry original art to member groups and towns throughout Virginia. Exhibitions are sent to schools, clubs, libraries. The lively arts of drama, dance and music are presented in the Museum Theater.

Richmond

A PHOTOGRAPHER attempting to get a particular scene in any large city has to maneuver his camera to avoid offensive advertising signs, overhead wires, traffic signs and the ever-present automobile. I had my share of troubles in Richmond in trying to photograph Monumental Church (Page 100) without having signs, wires and automobiles detract from the picture. On my third attempt I waited four-and-a-half hours. (And some people think that taking pictures is just a matter of snapping the shutter!) I waited that long to get a view free of parked cars. Sometimes there would be two vacant spots in front of the church, but a third would have a car in it. Finally, just when I was ready to quit for the day, all three parking spots became empty.

I passed the time by consulting maps and guide books to plan my pictures for the following day or talking to passersby. Many would stop to watch what I was doing and then invariably they would ask, "What're you photographing?" When I told them some would then ask, "Why? That church has been there for a 100 years."

Ampthill (Page 98) and Wilton (Page 99) are lovely houses and both remarkable in that they have been carefully moved from their original locations. I have been in both and I think that their interiors are magnificent.

The Confederate Museum (Page 97) and St. John's Church (Page 100) are not made from conventional angles. The angles I selected were difficult to shoot but I think they make more interesting studies.

The Richmond skyline (Page 96) was one of the last pictures I made for the book. It was made with infra-red film for more clarity and was shot with a 300 MM lens.

A. A. B.

RICHMOND . . . Capital of Virginia since 1779, Richmond is a charming blend of the old and the new. The town was laid out in 1737 and before long it was a metropolis of the old South. Today it is a financial, industrial, commercial and educational center of the new South. It has a metropolitan population of approximately 500,000. Sky- scrapers have risen on its seven ancient hills. Some 500 manufacturing plants turn out a variety of products— from cellophane to metal—valued at $1.5 billion annu- ally. Richmond's most important industry is the manu- facture of tobacco products. "Tobacco Row" produces 125 billion cigarettes annually.

DUPONT . . . The Spruance plant of the E. I. duPont de Nemours & Com- pany a few miles south of Richmond produces films and textile fibers. The plant is the world's largest producer of Nylon on a poundage basis. The film department makes cellophane, polyethylene and acetate films. The plant covers some 400 acres and em- ploys about 4,000. It has been in operation since 1929.

GLASGOW HOUSE . . . Ellen Glasgow, regarded as one of the most significant novelists of the South, lived here most of her life. She was born in 1874 and died in 1945. She wrote more than 20 novels that dealt with Virginia and its people; her novel "In This Our Life" won the Pulitzer Prize in 1942.

JOHN MARSHALL HOUSE . . . The house was designed and built around 1789 by Chief Justice Marshall who lived here until his death in 1835. As Chief Justice he made precedent-setting conservative decisions for 34 years. The house is now occupied by the Association for the Preservation of Virginia Antiquities.

CONFEDERATE MUSEUM . . . Built in 1818, the mansion was bought and furnished by the Confederacy as a "worthy White House" for Jefferson Davis and his family. Winnie Davis, "Daughter of the Confederacy," was born here. It is now a museum and it houses the world's largest collection of Confederate relics. They include the original Constitution of the Confederate states, the original Great Seal and Robert E. Lee's sword.

AMPTHILL . . . Originally this house, above, stood on the south bank of the James five miles below Richmond. It was probably built about 1732. The name comes from Ampthill Castle in England. The house, which was dismantled and moved to Richmond in 1929-30, is one of the outstanding colonial residences in Virginia.

WICKHAM-VALENTINE HOUSE . . . The house, below left, was built in 1812 for John Wickham and is an outstanding example of Federal architecture. It was later owned by Mann S. Valentine II who left it as a public museum. The museum, concentrating on the life and history of Richmond, is mainly in adjoining buildings.

POE MUSEUM . . . The cottage was built about 1686 and is called the oldest house in Richmond. Scratched on front wall are initials "J.R.," believed to be initials of "Jacobus Rex," James II, King of England. The house and garden are part of a shrine to Edgar Allan Poe who lived and worked in the area for years. On exhibition are Poe memorabilia and other objects associated with his life in Richmond.

CABELL HOUSE . . . This Monument Avenue house was the home for many years of James Branch Cabell (1879-1958) who wrote more than 30 books, including satirical fiction and essays. His most famous book was "Jurgen," published in 1919. In 1929, at the age of 50, and after publishing 20 books, the author dropped James from his name and, as Branch Cabell, began a new literary career.

WILTON . . . This is the only known house in the United States panelled from floor to ceiling in every room, hall and closet. It was built by William Randolph, III about 1750 on the north bank of the James, six miles below Richmond. Because it was surrounded by expanding industry, the Colonial Dames of America in the State of Virginia bought Wilton in 1933 and removed it to Richmond where it sits on a bluff above the James. The Garden Club of Virginia planted the grounds with large box, holly hedges and willow oaks.

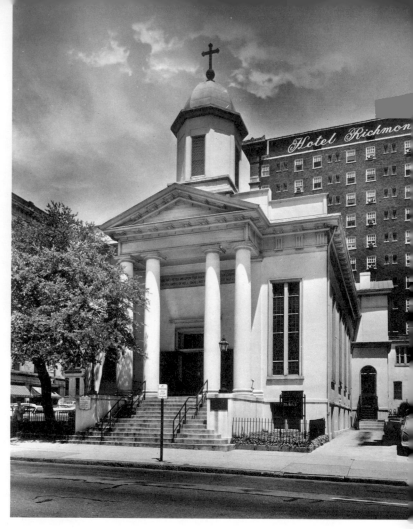

ST. JOHN'S . . . This Episcopal church is one of the oldest wooden buildings in Virginia. It was built in 1741 and has been enlarged several times. The second Virginia Convention met here March 20, 1775 and heard Patrick Henry make his famous "liberty or death" speech. Poe's mother is buried in the churchyard.

ST. PETER'S AND MONUMENTAL . . . St. Peter's Catholic Church, above, was erected in 1835 and was the cathedral church of Richmond diocese until 1906. Monumental Church, below, was built in 1814, memorializing the 72 victims of the Richmond Theater fire of 1811. Lafayette, Poe and Marshall worshipped here.

HOLLYWOOD CEMETERY . . . Named for its magnificent holly trees, this cemetery overlooks the James. Among those buried here are Presidents James Monroe and John Tyler (his stone is on the left, above), Jefferson Davis, John Randolph of Roanoke, Douglas Southall Freeman, Ellen Glasgow and James Branch Cabell.

SHOCKOE HILL CEMETERY . . . Sheltered by ancient elms and magnolias and enclosed by a brick wall, Shockoe Hill Cemetery was used chiefly between 1825 and 1875. Chief Justice John Marshall and his family lie in the lot shown below. Also here is the grave of Elizabeth Van Lew, a Union spy, marked with an unusual stone.

101

REYNOLDS METALS . . . This aluminum building in Richmond is headquarters for the Reynolds Metals Company, a nationwide organization of 35 plants. In 1958 two professors of the University of Virginia made a survey of Virginia architecture, sponsored by the Virginia Museum of Fine Arts, to determine the twelve most outstanding buildings from the close of the Revolutionary War. The Reynolds building was one of their selections.

FEDERAL BUILDING . . . This twelve-story structure is the largest office building in Richmond. It was designed to centralize and house under one roof seventeen Federal agencies. More than 1,300 government employees work here. The contemporary style building of vertical blocks was designed by two Richmond architectural firms. It cost $8,590,000, and stands at 400 North Eighth Street.

CENTENNIAL CENTER . . . The domed building was the focus of Virginia's five-year Civil War Centennial program. Its films and exhibits interpreted the story of the Civil War in Virginia—where 60 per cent of the fighting took place. It has been converted into a student center for the Medical College of Virginia.

U. OF RICHMOND . . . The University of Richmond embraces Richmond College (for men) and Westhampton College (for women). It has an enrollment of about 4,000. The university traces its beginnings to the Virginia Baptist Seminary which was incorporated as Richmond College in 1840. In 1914 the college moved out to Westhampton, a Richmond suburb. Six years later it was chartered as a university. The Boatright Memorial Library is pictured.

APPOMATTOX MANOR . . . Gen. U. S. Grant used Appomattox Manor, above, as his headquarters during the siege of Petersburg. Lincoln stopped here while waiting for Richmond to fall. In 1967 legislation was introduced in Congress to enable the Interior Department to acquire the plantation near Hopewell.

TUCKAHOE . . . The frame dwelling shown below stands on the James River, thirteen miles west of Richmond. It was built by William Randolph or his son Thomas, around 1710. On the grounds is a brick schoolhouse in which Thomas Jefferson received part of his early education. The estate has an elaborate box-labyrinth.

RANDOLPH-MACON . . . Founded in 1830, through the efforts of the Methodist Church, Randolph-Macon is, by date of charter, the oldest Methodist-related college in America. It is a liberal arts college for men with an enrollment of about 700. The college is in Ashland, twelve miles north of Richmond. Blackwell Auditorium, above, is one of eleven new buildings erected during the past decade.

EGYPTIAN BUILDING . . . This was the first permanent building of the Medical College of Virginia. It was built in 1845 and restored in 1939. It is considered the purest example of Egyptian architecture in the U.S. today. Note the mummy case design of the fence posts and the obelisks at the entrance. MCV has one of the largest medical plants in the South. There are about 1,500 students in its schools of medicine, dentistry, pharmacy and nursing. It operates four hospitals.

UNIVERSITY OF VIRGINIA . . . Since its founding in 1819, the University of Virginia has borne the impress of its creator, Thomas Jefferson, who planned its early curriculum as well as its grounds and original buildings. Opposite is the Rotunda, a modified reproduction of the Pantheon at Rome. It was "Mr. Jefferson's Pet" and was intended to become the focal point of the University. On either side of it, above, are two rows of pavilions used as residences for professors. They are connected by one-story colonnades behind which are student rooms, reserved for honor men. The area between is known as the Lawn. The Grounds cover more than 700 acres. Over 8,400 students attend the University at Charlottesville. The Honor System has been student controlled since 1842.

Piedmont

DURING the last 30 years I have visited 48 of the 50 states. None of these can offer the diversity of scenery and history that Virginia has—an ocean shoreline, the fabulous Chesapeake which is fed by many rivers and streams, green mountains and great valleys, and a unique culture that goes back over 300 years. (The only state that approaches it is Maryland, my native state.)

Often I'm asked what town in Virginia impresses me the most. Without hesitating I always reply, "Fredericksburg." The local Chamber of Commerce proclaims it as Virginia's "most historic town." For once I agree wholeheartedly with local boosters. The town has historic shrines, elegant houses, a lovely setting on the Rappahannock River—coupled with the grace of centuries and unforgettable charm.

Great Falls (Page 110) may disappear if the Potomac River is dammed to provide more water for Washington and the growing communities in the surrounding area. So too would White's Ferry (Page 115). This is the last of many ferries that crossed the Potomac. It's an unusual experience to use this ancient method of crossing a great river—and yet be only minutes from the capital of the United States, which prides itself on its technological achievements.   A. A. B.

DULLES AIRPORT . . . This was the country's first airport designed for jet planes. It covers 10,000 acres in Fairfax and Loudoun Counties and in terms of acreage is the largest in the U.S. The terminal building was designed by Eero Saarinen. Its concrete roof hangs like a great canvas hammock on steel cables between rows of concrete columns. The giant mobile lounges in the foreground carry passengers from the terminal out to the waiting planes. The international airport was dedicated in November, 1962. It is 27 miles southwest of Washington.

FAIRFAX STATION . . . Clara Barton, founder of the American Red Cross, helped care for the wounded at Fairfax Station early in September, 1862 after the second battle of Manassas and action near Chantilly. This is St. Mary's Catholic Church; it stands on Route 123, south of Fairfax.

FOXCROFT . . . Author Cleveland Amory called Foxcroft "perhaps the foremost of America's private girls' schools." It is situated on 600 acres in the Piedmont Valley near Middleburg. Miss Charlotte Haxall Noland founded the school in Brick House, above, in 1914. The mother of George Washington is said to have lived here as a girl.

MIDDLEBURG HUNT . . . One of the most noted hunts in America is the Middleburg Hunt, established in 1906 and recognized in 1908. It has 25 couples of American hounds and hunts three days a week from November 1 through March 15. It ranges over an area, 10 by 15 miles, of beautiful rolling countryside.

GREAT FALLS . . . Here the Potomac plunges 76 feet over a chaos of rock through a mile of gorge to create some of the wildest "white water" in the East. Bordering the Virginia side of the river is Great Falls Park. It is open all year and is noted for its trees, birds and plants. Nearby are the remains of the Potowmack Canal, first in the nation and forerunner of the Chesapeake and Ohio Canal. George Washington planned the Potowmack waterway which had five short canals with locks to bypass the falls and rapids. Construction began in 1785.

MILTON'S FORD . . . On the night of June 3, 1781, Jack Jouett started out from the Cuckoo Tavern in Louisa County to warn Thomas Jefferson at Monticello and members of the Virginia assembly at Charlottesville of an approaching British force that was sent to capture them. This is the ford over the Rivanna River where young Jouett is believed to have crossed near the end of his now famous ride of some 40 miles over back-country roads. In his writings, Jefferson mentioned using this ford.

CUMBERLAND C. H. . . . The courthouse for Cumberland County stands in Cumberland and was erected in 1818. Its brick walls were laid in an unusual bonding and the windows contain old rippled panes of glass. A small bell hangs from the center of the portico. The county was named for Prince William, the Duke of Cumberland.

MONTEBELLO . . . This Orange County mansion is considered to be one of the most beautiful in the Piedmont country. It has been occupied by members of the same family since it was built by slave labor in 1740. It has been enlarged several times. In 1862-63 the grounds were used for an encampment by Gen. Robert E. Lee's army and Lee and his staff were entertained in the house.

BOOKER T. WASHINGTON . . . This cabin is a reproduction of the one in which Booker T. Washington was born a slave April 5, 1856 on a small plantation. After his emancipation he worked his way through school and was graduated from Hampton Institute, where he later taught. He founded Tuskegee Institute in Alabama, became an adviser of Presidents, author of thirteen books and a recognized leader of his race. His birthplace, sixteen miles east of Rocky Mount, was established as a national monument in 1957.

111

MARY WASHINGTON . . . Mary Washington is the Woman's College of the University of Virginia and is the largest woman's college in Virginia. It has an enrollment of over 2,000. The grounds, comprising 381 acres, are on Marye's Heights overlooking Fredericksburg. Within sight of the hill are the home and tomb of Mary Washington, the president's mother. Above is the Fine Arts Center, three separate buildings connected by arches.

FREDERICKSBURG . . . The building where James Monroe practiced law from 1786 to 1790, below left, stands in the heart of Fredericksburg. It contains many Monroe pieces, including the desk on which he wrote the message which became known as the Monroe Doctrine. The Masonic Lodge, below right, is as active today as it was when George Washington "entered apprentice" in the 1750's. The Bible on which he was sworn is on exhibit.

KENMORE . . . This handsome mansion was built in 1752 by Col. Fielding Lewis, a Revolutionary patriot, for his bride, Betty, only sister of George Washington. The 863-acre estate was surveyed by Washington, and it is said that Kenmore became closer to him than any other place with the exception of Mount Vernon. The Fredericksburg house was purchased in the 1920's by the Kenmore Association whose members have made it into one of the outstanding museum houses in the United States.

JACKSON SHRINE . . . Accidentally shot by his own men, Gen. Stonewall Jackson was first taken to Wilderness Tavern, then brought to this house, near Guinea Station, which was out of the war zone. Jackson died here May 10, 1863. The house, not far from Fredericksburg, is maintained by the National Park Service.

APOTHECARY SHOP . . . On the advice of George Washington, a close friend, Dr. Hugh Mercer settled in Fredericksburg. He practiced medicine and set up his apothecary shop in this building. Washington kept a desk here for transacting business when he was in town. A large collection of apothecary bottles and implements are on display.

PEAKS OF OTTER . . . The two peaks are Flat Top, right, with an altitude of 4,001 feet, and Sharp Top, left, altitude 3,870. The Virginia stone for the Washington Monument was taken from Sharp Top. A sightseeing bus runs up to its summit. The Peaks are on the Blue Ridge Parkway, which connects with the Skyline Drive.

WHEAT FIELD . . . Large fields with shocks of grain are fairly rare sights. Many farmers are using more modern methods to harvest crops. This farm is in Loudoun County. Virginia produces around 6,000,000 bushels of wheat a year; average yield per acre is about 27 bushels. About half of Virginia is still farm land.

GREEN FIELDS, ROCK WALLS . . . Livestock, poultry and dairying provide more than half of Virginia's farm income. In 1960 cash receipts from these sources were around $253,000,000. The dry walls of stone which fence the meadow are common in Fauquier County where this peaceful scene was photographed.

WHITE'S FERRY . . . The *Gen. Jubal Early* is a converted military landing barge which crosses the Potomac at White's Ferry, near Leesburg. It operates from 6 A.M. to 10 P.M. The sign says the ferry can be summoned by sounding horn or flashing lights. It is the last of many ferries that once crossed the river.

WATERFORD . . . Founded in 1733, Waterford was once a busy trading and manufacturing center. During the Industrial Revolution it came close to being a deserted village. In the last few years the Loudoun County town has been rediscovered, largely by urbanites who are carefully restoring the old houses and stores.

TOUCHES OF THE PAST . . . The Indiantown mill is tucked into the woods beside a dirt road near Locust Grove. Built in 1845, it still grinds corn in an old-fashioned way. The miller receives one-eighth of the milling as his fee. Below, a blacksmith works at his trade in Altavista. Old smithies have virtually disappeared.

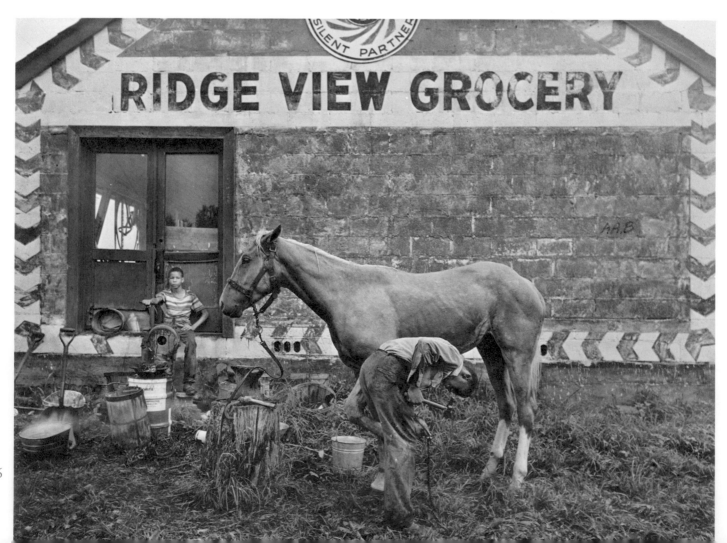
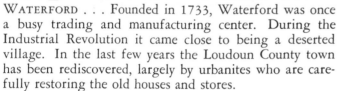

FOX HUNTING . . . "The Hound and Horn country," in the words of a Virginia writer, "is that green gently rolling portion of northern Virginia in which hunting is never out of season." "Horse Country" includes Clarke, Loudoun, Fairfax, and Fauquier counties and parts of Rappahannock, Culpeper, Orange and Albemarle. Best known hunts are Blue Ridge, Casanova, Fairfax, Farm-ington, Keswick, Loudoun, Middleburg, Montpelier, Old Dominion, Orange County, Piedmont and Warrenton. The pictures are of Orange County, established in 1903. The hunt is named after Orange County, N.Y. because so many of the original members came from there. Its kennels are at The Plains, Fauquier County, which is the center of Virginia's foxhunting.

VIRGINIA GOLD CUP . . . The Virginia Gold Cup Race is one of the country's outstanding steeplechases and attracts racing devotees from all over the East. It is run on the first Saturday in May over the Broadview estate near Warrenton. The race was started in 1922 and is run under the auspices of the Warrenton Hunt.

UP AND OVER . . . The Virginia Gold Cup course is four miles in length over rolling country with 22 heavy chestnut rail fences standing an average height of three feet, ten inches. The Cup itself is a thistle-shaped goblet with horse and bird motifs. It was made from gold mined in California during the Gold Rush.

ANCIENT SPORT . . . Foxhunting has been popular in Northern Virginia since the middle of the 18th century. Dr. Thomas Walker imported a pack of hounds from England in 1742 and became master of the Castle Hill hounds. The oldest pack in the United States is Piedmont which was established in 1840 as a private pack. Foxhunting was the favorite sport of several Presidents; Washington devoted much of his spare time to the chase.

BROOKMEADE FARMS . . . For many years this farm was owned and operated by Mrs. Isabel Dodge Sloane who raced Brookmeade Stable. Many horses that helped make that stable the leading money winner of American racing in 1934 and 1950 were raised here, including *Sword Dancer*, horse of the year in 1959. The 777-acre farm near Upperville is now owned by William C. Crossman Jr. It has an estimated 28 miles of fences.

FIRST HORSE SHOW . . . The Upperville Colt and Horse Show was organized in 1853, and is the oldest such show in the U.S. The show grounds are in a grove of beautiful oak trees and the management has contrived to lay out the rings and paddocks around the trees. The show is held in June and several hundred top horses are always entered.

THE SHENANDOAH . . . Bordering the beautiful and lush Shenandoah Valley on the west are the Shenandoah Mountains. Top, opposite page, is a view toward Reddish Knob which is 4,398 feet high. Above, near Bergton, in the northwest part of the state. Both of these scenes are in the George Washington National Forest which consists of 1,000,000 acres along the western side of Virginia, from the vicinity of Winchester on the north to the Covington area on the south. Bottom opposite page, a panorama of Blue Grass Valley, near Monterey.

Shenandoah Valley

SOME PICTURES are made on the spur of the moment, others take advance planning. Arrangements for the apple-picking picture (Page 130) were made weeks in advance. Boxes of apples were moved to a spot I had picked on the edge of a mountain and several men stood on makeshift scaffolding to push the loaded branches into the frame of my picture.

I was on the Skyline Drive when I noticed the storm sweeping up the valley. I jumped out of my car and recorded the scene on infra-red film (Page 132). This is one of the greatest natural sights I have ever shot.

Woodpeckers delayed the making of one picture; white street lines helped in making another. I had to go back to the Washington & Lee campus several times because workmen had a scaffold around the Washington statue. I found out they were repairing damage done by woodpeckers. The picture of Washington's office in Winchester (Page 129) should have been difficult because the view is always obstructed by cars. But the day I got there, there wasn't a car around—workmen were laying out new street lines.

Some will wonder why I selected the roadside stand (Page 135) instead of another shrine or house. The answer is simple: I'm fascinated by such stands and I think most tourists are, too. Furthermore, I think this is Americana in its purest form. A. A. B.

WINTER RESORT . . . The Homestead, with 17,000 acres in the Alleghenies at Hot Springs, has long been famous as a pleasant-weather resort with a variety of sports. It now features skiing from December to March on Warm Springs Mountain. A trestle-car lift, on the right above, carries skiers to the top of the 3,200-foot slope, which has a 500-foot drop. There are two miles of slopes and trails. If snow doesn't fall, it's machine-made with snow guns when the temperature is 30 degrees or below. This was developed on part of an old golf course.

NATURAL BRIDGE . . . The arch of stone was created by the action of water over millions of years. The bridge is 215 feet above Cedar Creek, 90 feet long and from 50 to 150 feet wide. U.S. Highway 11 runs across it. This great natural wonder was worshipped by the Indians as "the bridge of God." Young George Washington surveyed it about 1750 and climbed 23 feet up its side to carve his initials. Thomas Jefferson acquired the bridge and surrounding area from King George III in 1775 for 20 shillings. He built a cabin where he entertained visitors, including Henry Clay, James Monroe and John Marshall. The bridge is twelve miles south of Lexington.

VMI . . . Cadets of Virginia Military Institute, at Lexington, parade before a statue of "Stonewall" Jackson, who was a professor at the Institute. Founded in 1839, VMI is oldest state military college in the U.S. The cadet corps numbers 1,213. Gen. George C. Marshall, Gen. George S. Patton, Adm. Richard E. Byrd were VMI men.

BRIDGEWATER COLLEGE . . . The college was established in 1880 as Spring Creek Normal and Collegiate Institute. The name was changed to Bridgewater in 1889 and two years later it conferred its first degrees, becoming the first Church of the Brethren college ever to do so. The co-educational school, near Harrisonburg, has 700 students.

STAUNTON MILITARY ACADEMY . . . The Academy was founded in 1860 by William H. Kable. He and his son headed it for 60 years. It has 650 cadets who come from more than 30 states and twelve foreign countries. The Academy, situated on one of Staunton's hills, was first school in the South rated as an honor school by the Army.

WELCOME . . . Despite a snowstorm in the Shenandoah Mountains, Virginia offers a warm welcome to travelers. Its beautiful scenery and historic shrines attract such great number of visitors that tourism has become an important state wide business. On the sign are the state bird and flower: the cardinal and American dogwood.

MARY BALDWIN . . . Mary Baldwin College in Staunton, above, was founded in 1842 as Augusta Female Seminary by Rufus W. Bailey, a minister and educator from Maine. It has about 500 students, and is the oldest senior college for women of the Presbyterian Church in the U.S. Shown are a dormitory, activities building and dining hall.

RANDOLPH-MACON WOMAN'S COLLEGE . . . This Methodist-related liberal arts college was opened in 1893. It was the first woman's college south of the Potomac to be granted a Phi Beta Kappa charter. The school, which has an enrollment of 725 from more than 35 states, is in Lynchburg. The Herbert C. Lipscomb Library is shown.

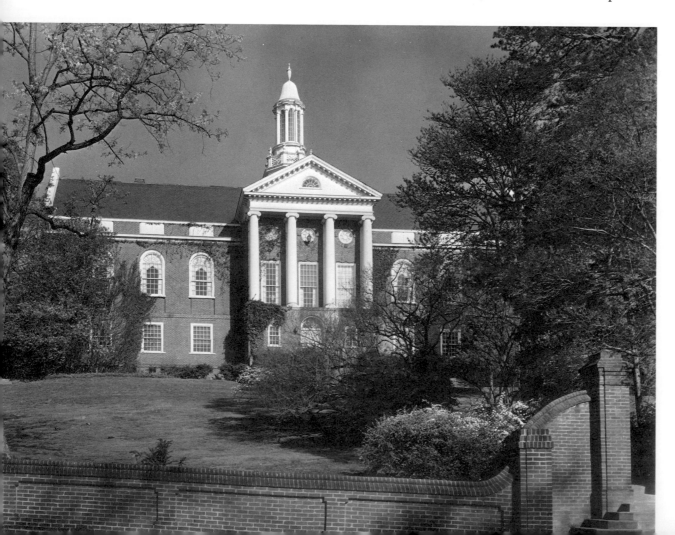

WASHINGTON AND LEE . . . White columns are the architectural symbol of Washington and Lee University at Lexington, above. Founded in 1749, it was later named in honor of Washington who made a generous gift and Robert E. Lee who served as president. Lee said, "We have but one rule: our students are gentlemen."

MADISON COLLEGE . . . Founded in 1908 as a normal school, the name was changed in 1938 to honor the fourth president of U.S. Madison is a state-aided liberal arts school and its major function is to prepare teachers for Virginia public schools. The college, in Harrisonburg, has an enrollment of about 1,800, mostly women.

127

HEBRON CHURCH . . . This church was built about 1740 but its origins go back to 1725. Hebron was founded by Germans who settled in Madison County in 1724. It is the oldest Lutheran church in the South, possibly in the country. The church, recently restored, has an organ built about 1800 which is considered one of the first in America. It was hauled to the church at Madison by ox cart.

OLD CHAPEL . . . This Clarke County chapel was built in 1796 and has always been called Old Chapel. It was built of native limestone and, except for necessary repairs, has remained unchanged. Boulders in front of the church were placed there years ago for the convenience of women riders. The chapel now is used only for burial services and an annual service on the second Sunday in September.

SARATOGA . . . General Daniel Morgan built Saratoga in 1781 and named it after the Revolutionary War Battle that made him famous. He used Hessian soldiers from Burgoyne's captured army to build the house of block and quarried limestone. The outside walls are almost two feet thick. Saratoga is near Millwood in Clarke County.

WASHINGTON'S OFFICE . . . This building in Winchester was used by young George Washington from time to time between 1749-53 while he was surveying Lord Fairfax's vast holdings. He also used it while he was supervising the erection of Fort Loudoun in 1756-57. A small museum is maintained on the premises.

FESTIVAL . . . One of the country's best known salutes to Spring is the Shenandoah Apple Blossom Festival in Winchester the first week in May. The three-day festival includes gigantic parades, a pageant, special shows, a grand ball and the coronation of Queen Shenandoah, always a beauty and often the daughter of well-known parents. This queen is pictured in an appropriate setting of apple blossoms.

WEEMS BOTTOM . . . Known as the Mount Jackson or Weems Bottom covered bridge, this spans the North Fork of the Shenandoah in Shenandoah County on Route 720, west of U.S. Route 11. It was built in 1893 and is 191 feet long. The Burr truss bridge is still in use and is one of nine remaining covered bridges in Virginia.

OLD HUMPBACK . . . Oldest and most famous of Virginia's covered bridges, and only one of its kind in U.S. It has a rise of eight feet from each end to the center. Built in 1835 of hand-hewn oak timbers and locust pins, it was open until 1929. Now used only for foot traffic, it is about three miles west of Covington.

APPLES . . . Virginia grows about 10,000,000 bushels of apples annually. Pictured at left is one of Senator Harry F. Byrd's eleven orchards. He had 200,000 trees planted on 4,000 acres and he grew about 1,250,000 bushels a year. This, the largest non-corporation apple operation in the U.S., is now run by the family.

FALLING SPRING . . . "The only remarkable cascade in this country," Thomas Jefferson wrote, "is that of Falling Spring . . . It falls over a rock 200 feet into the valley. This cataract will bear no comparison with that of Niagara, as to the quantity of water . . . but it is half as high again." The Spring is not far from Covington.

SKYLINE DRIVE . . . The famed Skyline Drive runs from Front Royal to Rockfish Gap, 105 miles along the crest of the Blue Ridge. This is typical of the magnificent panoramas from the Drive. Neighbor Mountain is on the right. The Drive runs through the 193,500-acre Shenandoah National Park, which is 75 miles long.

CAVERNS . . . Virginia has nine famous caverns. Battlefield dates from 1772, Bristol has different levels, Dixie has large rooms, Endless shows needle-like stalactites, Grand has a stalagmite 40 feet high, Luray is the largest, troops slept in Melrose, Shenandoah has "bacon-rinds" and Skyline features anthodites, flowers of mineral world.

132

McCormick Homestead . . . Working here Cyrus Hall McCormick perfected the mechanical grain reaper in 1831. By 1847, when he had sold nearly 800 reapers, McCormick moved west to the grain country. The house and many outbuildings have been restored. An original reaper is on exhibition. The homestead is near Raphine.

Pulpwood . . . The Bleached Board Division of the West Virginia Pulp and Paper Company at Covington consumes some 500,000 cords of hardwood a year. This is enough wood to pave a "log road" one foot deep, eight feet wide for about 1,400 miles. The Covington mill is one of the largest of its kind in the United States.

ROANOKE . . . Largest city in Virginia west of Richmond, Roanoke has a population of over 100,000. It is an important manufacturing, distribution and trade center. Products manufactured in its metropolitan area range from paper boxes to fire engines. The picture was made from Mill Mountain. The "world's largest man-made star" was erected on this mountain in 1949 as a symbol of the progressive spirit of Roanoke, which calls itself "Star City of the South."

WEAVER . . . W. C. Cook weaves rocker seats and all sizes of baskets in his Page Valley shop. He has been doing the work, almost a lost art, for 36 years. He uses thin strips of white oak which he shaves from logs. His only tools are an axe and knife.

STOP AND SHOP . . . Along all the highways traveled by tourists are such wayside displays. This one, on Pumpkin Hill, a few miles east of Luray, offers a wider range than most. On sale are woven baskets, pottery, chenille spreads, hand-hooked rugs, bird houses, woodcraft, souvenirs and cold cider. Note the large totem pole.

"MASSA NUTTIN' " . . . Massanutten Mountain gets its name from an Indian word meaning "Indian basket." According to a Civil War story, when a Union general asked an old Negro "the name of that mountain" he replied, "Massa Nuttin' " because he thought that was the name. The high ridge, about 50 miles long, divides the upper Shenandoah Valley. The middle photograph was made from the town of Shenandoah; Page Valley in the foreground is under a blanket of snow. Lower picture is another view of Massanutten, west of Luray.

ROLLING FIELDS . . . Corn grows on more than five times as much land as tobacco in Virginia. In recent years the annual crop has been about 32,000,000 bushels. The state has more than 100,000 farms and the average one is about 135 acres in size. This attractive farm is in Augusta County on Route 42, just a few miles from Moscow.

NATURAL CHIMNEYS . . . The seven chimneys range from 67 to 107 feet in height. The one on the left leans 13.5 feet, about as much as the Tower of Pisa. The chimneys, which stand at Mt. Solon in the Shenandoah Valley, are made of limestone and are an estimated 500,000,000 years old. There are nature-made tunnels in the bases.

"TURKEY CAPITAL" . . . Rockingham is the largest turkey producing county in the nation, raising 18,000,000 annually. Rockingham is rated among the country's 100 leading agricultural counties and its annual $30,000,000 production is the best in Virginia. These are Broad Whites; at market they will weigh about 24 pounds.

MENNONITE COUNTRY . . . Six buggies with Mennonites roll down a country road near Dayton on the way to Sunday worship. The men wear plain clothing with black broad-brimmed hats and beards. Women wear large plain bonnets and long full dresses of solid color. The foot washing service is still observed by old order Mennonites.

DEAD CENTER . . . The geographical center of Virginia is in Buckingham County, close to Mt. Rush which is at the junction of U.S. Route 60 and State Route 24. The state contains 40,815 square miles, including 977 miles of inland water. The greatest distance east to west is 425 miles, north to south, 205 miles.

LAST CAPITAL . . . Danville became the "Last Capital of the Confederacy" from April 3 to 10, 1865, when this mansion was occupied by Jefferson Davis and his cabinet after the evacuation of Richmond. Here Davis called his last full cabinet meeting, issued his last official proclamation and received the news of Lee's surrender at Appomattox. The mansion at the time was the home of Major W. T. Sutherlin. It is now the Public Library.

RED HILL . . . Patrick Henry termed Red Hill, which is near Brookneal on a bluff overlooking the Staunton River, the "garden spot of the world." He bought the property about 1794 and moved there permanently two years later. He died at Red Hill in 1799. His grave is marked, "His fame his best epitaph." The main house was destroyed by fire. It and the adjoining kitchen were restored by the Patrick Henry Memorial Foundation which purchased the 900-acre property. Henry's law office and Henry's tree still stand. There is a beautiful boxwood garden.

South Side

ON PAGE 138 is a picture of the geographical center of Virginia. I wondered how this was determined so I investigated. It is done in a simple yet ingenious way. The U.S. Geological Survey cuts a templet from stiff cardboard in the shape of the state and balances it on a fine point. The point marks the center—it's as easy at that.

All of the tobacco grown during colonial times was planted on tidewater farms. This is no longer true. I don't know of a single patch of tobacco growing in tidewater today that can't be covered by a blanket.

The picture of the quarry on Page 145 could not be made with an ordinary camera and lens. I had to have a wide-angle lens to get the width of the quarry and yet I had to keep my background sharp enough to show the men in the lift. With the exception of the aerial photography, most of the pictures in this book were made by a five-by-seven Linhof view camera with a group of nine lenses, ranging from 80 to 500 MM.

When I made the cotton picture (Page 144) there wasn't a cloud in the sky. The picture badly needed clouds. Rather than wait, perhaps days, for the right clouds I superimposed some from another negative when I printed the cotton picture. I have several hundred negatives in my cloud file.　　　　A. A. B.

BREMO . . . Thomas Jefferson was consulted in the design of this mansion. He recommended two men who had worked on Monticello and one of them drew up the final plans. The house was started about 1815 and completed in 1820. The recessed porch, above, faces the James. The estate is in Fluvanna County.

HAMPDEN-SYDNEY . . . Founded in 1776, Hampden-Sydney is the second oldest college in Virginia and the tenth oldest in the country. Affiliated with the Presbyterian Church, it is a liberal arts school for men with an enrollment of 500. President William Henry Harrison was a graduate. The 400-acre campus is near Farmville.

SWEET BRIAR . . . This independent residential college for women, above, has a 3,000-acre campus in the foothills of the Blue Ridge near Lynchburg. It was chartered in 1901. Sweet Briar administers the "Junior year in France" program, and has a special exchange with St Andrew's University, Scotland. It has 640 students.

LONGWOOD COLLEGE . . . The first teacher training institution for white teachers in Virginia, Longwood dates to 1884 when it was known as the State Female Normal School. The name was changed three times, finally becoming Longwood College in 1949. The college, for women, is in Farmville and has 1,100 students.

TOBACCO COUNTRY . . . Tobacco is grown in more than half of Virginia's 100 counties. There are four types: Flue-cured (also known as Bright), Burley (light air-cured), Fire-cured and Virginia "sun-cured." Flue-cured is the biggest crop. In recent years Virginia has produced about 130,000,000 pounds annually worth between $80,000,000 and $92,000,000. This is flue-cured.

TOBACCO HANDS . . . Tobacco is the most labor-demanding of all field crops. From seedbeds to harvest good tobacco depends on the care it gets. Some 64,300 farm families spend much of the year working the crop with the aid of some 250,000 seasonal workers. Flue tobacco grows best in sandy loams. Between 5,500 and 7,500 plants are set out per acre; the yield is up to 2,000 pounds.

"VIRGINIA" . . . Hands display tobacco on sticks outside a barn where it is flue-cured. Flues conduct heat into the tightly constructed barn, drying and treating the leaves and bringing them to the desired bright colors. Flue-cured tobacco is known throughout the world as "Virginia" and it is the chief ingredient of American cigarettes. This farm is in Pittsylvania County.

TOBACCO AUCTION . . . Danville is one of the world's largest tobacco markets for the sale and handling of flue-cured tobacco. There are more than 1,000,000 square feet of auction warehouse floor space at Danville, where this picture was made. Auction sales take place in about eighteen communities. The marketing season usually begins late in September and ends in February.

COTTON . . . Once a major farm enterprise in Virginia, cotton is now of relatively minor importance. In recent years the crop has ranged between 4,000 and 12,200 bales. Because of the small fields, cotton is still picked by hand. It is grown in fourteen counties. The biggest producers are Greensville and Southampton.

WORLD'S LARGEST . . . Dan River Mills is the largest single-unit textile mill in the world. The company employs some 10,500 people in Danville to operate 9,000 looms and 450,000 spindles. Danville, with a population of more than 46,000, is an industrial city spread over hills that slope toward a big bend in the Dan River.

CAMP PICKETT . . . Troops line the airport runway for a review at the 46,000-acre army post near Blackstone. The camp is used during the summer by 3,000 to 4,000 troops from National Guard and reserve units for training with tanks, artillery and ordnance. The camp was first opened in 1942. It has 30 miles of tank trails.

SLATE QUARRY . . . Quarries centered around the town of Arvonia produce a slate which is known for its excellent durability as well as its beauty and versatility. Because of its distinctive qualities it is sold under the copyrighted name Buckingham slate. The quarries date to the late 1700's and have been in continuous use since. Many of them are 200 feet deep. The deepest is 350 feet. Note the two men being pulled up in the cage at the rear of the quarry.

145

CUMBERLAND GAP . . . Through this natural gap in the Alleghenies—discovered in 1750—ran the Wilderness Road, main artery for the great trans-Allegheny migration which won the Northwest Territory and extended the western boundary of the U.S. to the Mississippi. The camera is in Tennessee, Kentucky is on the left, Virginia on the right. Below, Chatham Hill Gully.

25,000-ACRE "RANCH" . . . Cowboys drive a herd of Herefords, opposite page, on the "ranch" of the Stuart Land and Cattle Company, which consists of 25,000 acres. largest Hereford operation east of the Mississippi. There are 3,300 Herefords, 3,000 sheep and 1,000 hogs on the "ranch," which has 50 employees, including several cowboys. Center of the operation is at Rosedale.

The Southwest

AFTER TRAVELING through much of Virginia's 40,000 square miles, I discovered that its Southwest is an area unknown to many Virginians. When I talked to the editor of a weekly paper in that corner of the state he expressed delight that someone was finally portraying his beloved and beautiful country. "People in Richmond don't know what goes on down here," he remarked. He went on to say that nine state capitals are closer to Cumberland Gap than it is to Richmond. I checked up and found these capitals are closer: Charleston, W. Va., Raleigh, N. C., Columbia, S. C., Atlanta, Ga., Columbus, Ohio, Indianapolis, Ind., Frankfort, Ky., Nashville, Tenn., and Montgomery, Ala.

I had more difficulty in finding Mount Rogers, the highest point in Virginia, than any other place. If this sounds ridiculous keep in mind that many mountains rise gradually over an area of many miles. Whenever I thought I was within camera range of the top, a dozen ridges would appear to be of equal height. It seemed that no two natives would agree on the highest ridge. I finally got the summit; it's pictured on Page 149.

For sheer beauty, far removed from sights and sounds of civilization, I must single out Abrams Falls (Page 151). If you want to see it, be prepared for an arduous trip. You will need the agility of a young mountain goat to climb some of the cliffs along the stream.　　A. A. B.

TROUT FISHING—SHOT TOWER . . . An angler tries his luck in Big Laurel Creek. Virginia has 135 mountain streams with brook and rainbow trout. The shot tower, top right, at Jackson's Ferry, Wythe County, was built about 1820. Shot was made by pouring molten lead through a sieve which hardened into pellets as it fell.

MOUNTAIN MUSIC . . . Throughout the southwestern part of Virginia, country people gather to play and sing mountain music—hymns and ballads, some old, some new. Such music can be heard at the Virginia Highlands Festival at Abingdon during the first two weeks of August and also at the Old Fiddlers' Convention at Galax.

"VIRGINIA CREEPER" . . . This famous mixed train (passengers and freight) of the Norfolk and Western ran between Abingdon and West Jefferson, N.C., until 1962, winding through remote and beautiful mountain country and crossing 108 bridges on its 55½-mile trip. Special excursions, with diesel power, are still made.

HIGHEST POINT . . . Mt. Rogers, rising 5,719 feet, is the highest point in Virginia and one of the highest east of the Mississippi. It is in Smyth and Grayson counties and is the responsibility of the National Forest Service. The more than mile-high summit holds the last remnant of a "glacial front forest" in Virginia.

NATURAL WONDERS . . . High above Rt. 421 and the Powell River, near Pennington Gap, is an immense rock jutting out from the mountain, and the rock has the distinct profile of a head and neck. The rock is known today as "Old Stone Face." A railroad tunnel runs through the "neck." In Scott county, fourteen miles from Gate City, is the Natural Tunnel, left, through which railroad tracks and Stock Creek run. The tunnel is about 100 feet in diameter and some 900 feet in length. It is now within a State Park.

ABRAMS FALLS . . . Southwest Virginia's highest waterfall, opposite page, is on Abrams Creek, west of Abingdon and near the village of Wallace. The water falls almost 70 feet and then falls almost 40 feet more. The stream is about 20 feet wide. It is between Three Springs and the North Fork of the Holston River in Washington county.

VPI . . . Virginia Polytechnic Institute was founded in 1872. It had one building, a faculty of four and 132 students. Now it is one of the largest centers of learning in Virginia with an enrollment of about 8,900. VPI has five schools: agriculture, business, engineering, home economics, science and general studies. It is noted for its research and extension work. The campus is at Blacksburg.

HOLLINS COLLEGE . . .Founded in 1842, Hollins was the first chartered school for young women in Virginia. Once known as Valley Union Seminary, the name was changed to Hollins College in 1911. The liberal arts college, with 700 students, has special academic programs, including foreign study. The Jessie Ball duPont chapel, below, is the newest building on the 400-acre campus near Roanoke.

RADFORD . . . Radford College is the Woman's Division of Virginia Polytechnic Institute. The college dates to 1910 when it was established as a state normal school; it became affiliated with VPI in 1944. It has about 2,000 students and most are training to be teachers. The 70-acre campus of the state-supported institution is in the residential section of the city of Radford, 40 miles west of Roanoke. The John Preston McConnell Library is in the foreground.

EMORY & HENRY . . . Founded in 1836 by the Methodist Church, Emory & Henry was named in honor of Bishop John Emory, a hero of Methodism, and Patrick Henry, patriot and orator. It is the "senior college" of the Mountain Empire section of Virginia. This coeducational liberal arts college is situated on a 150-acre campus at Emory and has an enrollment of about 750 students.

ROANOKE COLLEGE . . . This small, independent liberal arts college for men and women traces its beginnings to the Virginia Institute which was established in 1842 at Mt. Tabor. Chartered as Roanoke College in 1853, it has always been affiliated with the Lutheran Church. The college, situated in Salem since 1847, has an enrollment of about 750. The Administration Building is shown.

153

RIPSHIN AND GROUNDHOG . . . Sherwood Anderson lived at Ripshin Farm, above, during the summer from 1925 until his death in 1941. He built the house himself with stones and timber from the farm. Ripshin, near Marion, is now used as a retreat by artists and writers who were friends of Anderson. Above right, Groundhog Overlook near the Virginia line on the Blue Ridge Parkway, which serves as a scenic connecting link between the Shenandoah National Park of Virginia and the Great Smoky Mountains National Park of North Carolina and Tennessee. At the overlook are examples of chestnut rail fences.

BARTER THEATRE . . . In 1932, during the depression, Robert Porterfield and a group of unemployed New York actors opened the Barter Theatre in Abingdon, a summer resort in the Virginia Highlands. Anything edible, from huckleberries to hams, was accepted as payment for tickets. The theatre has been going ever since. A number of famous actors have trained at Abingdon, including Gregory Peck. In 1946 it became the State Theatre of Virginia; the first state-subsidized theatre in America. Tickets are no longer bartered except for old customers. The theatre is open from June through September.

ON THE BLUE RIDGE . . . Mabry's Mill, south of Rocky Knob, still grinds corn meal and buckwheat flour by water power. A nearby self-guiding trail features old-time mountain industry. The log cabin, top right, was the home of Mrs. Orlean Hawks Pluckett from 1865 until her death in 1939 at the age of 104. She was a well-known midwife who helped deliver hundreds of babies in remote mountain cabins. Mill and cabin are on the Blue Ridge Parkway which follows the Blue Ridge Mountains for 355 miles at an average elevation of about 3,000 feet.

OFF THE BEATEN PATH . . . Benedict, right, is almost a ghost town. Once it was a prosperous community of 1,200 when the vast coal mines of the area were busy. Benedict is in Powell Valley, north of Pennington Gap. Below, a swinging bridge over the South Fork of the Powell River at Big Stone Gap. There are hundreds of these bridges in southwest Virginia and most are not as substantially built as this one.

LUMBER AND OIL . . . This sawmill is along Rt. 421 near Pennington Gap. Lumberman cut about 1,100,000,-000 board feet of timber a year for some 2,000 lumber mills. Top right, an oil rig at Ben Hur, in the far southwestern corner of Virginia. This is the only oil-producing area in the state; there are about 75 wells in the vicinity.

VIRGINIA'S LARGEST . . . The Clinch River plant of the Appalachian Power Company is the largest power station in Virginia. In 1960 it was rated the world's most efficient power plant. Clinch River can provide electric service for 1,000,000 homes. Near Carbo, in the heart of the coal fields, it consumes 1,800,000 tons a year.

COAL AND COAL MINERS . . . Virginia ranks among the leading coal-mining states, with about 30,300,000 tons a year. Most of the coal is bituminous and comes from the southwest counties of Buchanan, Dickenson, Wise, Russell and Tazewell. The first four account for about 95 per cent of Virginia's production. Above is a ramp operation, with an old mining camp on the other side of the tracks. The operator of the tipple buys from small independent truck miners and pays between $2.50 and $4 a ton. With a good vein and hard work an "independent" might mine 20 tons a day. Below, five Powell Valley miners rest outside a shaft.

SALTVILLE . . . Salt has been produced commercially in Saltville since about 1788. During the Civil War these deposits were the chief source of salt for the Confederacy. Abundant limestone in the immediate area facilitates the changing of sodium chloride into a variety of commercial products. The first shipments of soda ash were made in 1895 and since then the plant has run 24 hours a day, seven days a week, through wars and depression. Pump houses are shown.

WEAVER . . . An instructor weaves a rug at the June Tolliver House at Big Stone Gap, a non-profit organization where crafts of mountain life are taught. The heroine of the novel, "The Trail of the Lonesome Pine," lived here while she was going to school. The house contains classrooms, workshops and a craft and gift shop.

MOUNTAIN MOONSHINE . . . Federal agents destroy a mountain still, spilling mash down the mountain side. In 1962 Internal Revenue agents in Virginia seized 254 stills, 182,706 gallons of mash, 11,431 gallons of nontax-paid distilled spirits and 175 vehicles, and arrested 576 persons. Twenty years ago it wasn't unusual for agents to destroy over 1,000 stills a year.

FISH HATCHERY—MILLER . . . The Paint Bank National Fish Hatchery was established by the U.S. Bureau of Sport Fisheries and Wildlife to produce rainbow, brown and brook trout for stocking the waters of the George Washington and the Jefferson National Forests. Eggs are hatched in these long tanks. Below, a miller poses for his portrait in the Grant Wood manner at Glade Spring.

LARGEST MINE . . . A fossil tree some 200,000,000 years old is displayed at Moss No. 3, which says it is the world's largest coal mine. Operated by the Clinchfield Coal Co., the Dickenson County mine taps the largest single block of high grade metallurgical coal still left in the U.S. Of this reserve, 150,000,000 tons have been assigned to Moss No. 3, which produces some 5,100,000 tons a year.

FOSSIL TREE

THIS TREE GREW IN SOUTHWESTERN VIRGINIA ABOUT 200,000,000 YEARS AGO DURING THE GREATEST PERIOD OF COAL FORMATION THAT THE WORLD HAS EVER KNOWN. IT WAS RECOVERED WHILE STRIPPING THE CLINTWOOD (MOSS) COAL SEAM ON CLINCHFIELD PROPERTY IN DICKENSON COUNTY, VIRGINIA. IT IS A SPECIES OF LEPIDODENDRON WHOSE STUMPS ATTAINED DIAMETERS OF FROM 4 TO 6 FEET WITH TRUNKS REACHING HEIGHTS OF MORE THAN 100 FEET.

MANASSAS (BULL RUN) . . . Shortly after the firing on Fort Sumter, the North clamored for a quick move to capture Richmond and end the war. The plan was to move south through Fredericksburg. Across this overland route lay Manassas, an important railroad junction. Many curious civilians from Washington, carrying picnic baskets, accompanied the Federal troops, hoping to see a spectacle.

STONE BRIDGE . . . The Confederate forces were entrenched in an eight-mile line along Bull Run, a small stream about 26 miles southwest of Washington. The battle started at Stone Bridge. Partially destroyed during the war, the bridge was rebuilt and is now one of the principal landmarks of the battlefield. It stands beside Rt. 29 and has a triangular monument in the center.

HENRY'S FARM, FIRST MANASSAS

The Civil War

I HAD A wide variety of subject matter for this section as more than half of the battles between North and South took place on Virginia soil.

During the course of my work as a photographer, I've visited more than 50 battlefields in most of the states where the war was fought. With only a few exceptions, Virginia's battlefields are better preserved, better marked and better kept than any others. Trenches and redoubts are clearly visible, and there is an abundance of cannon to show where batteries stood. Few realize that the new carriages for these guns are made in a Virginia prison.

I carried three rifles with me and sometimes used them to give atmosphere to a scene. All are authentic. As a matter of fact, one belonged to my grandfather, Joel Goode Bodine, who lived in Bristow, Va., in the heart of the Manassas country.

Virginians might be interested in the comment of a well-known American on the intensity of fighting in Virginia compared to his state. While visiting Wilson Creek, Missouri, I had a terrible time trying to locate a specific battle area. When I returned home I wrote to Harry Truman and asked him why he didn't use his influence as a former President to have the battlefield properly marked and the beer cans removed. He answered by air mail and in typical fashion: "Our main trouble is that the people in charge of these things do not realize that the War was carried on just as viciously here, in fact more so, as it was in Virginia."   A .A. B.

STONE HOUSE . . . The best preserved landmark at Manassas is the Stone House. In the first major engagement of the Civil War, the Federal forces suffered disaster in a battle of mistakes. They were routed from the field and fled back to Washington in panic. The first "On-to-Richmond" drive was stopped. But the South failed to follow up its easy victory.

KERNSTOWN . . . The battle of Kernstown, fought on March 23, 1862, was the first in Stonewall Jackson's brilliant Valley campaign. His mission was to hold as many of the enemy in the area as possible, thus relieving pressure on the main Confederate army protecting Richmond. When Federal troops started to withdraw toward Washington, Jackson attacked at Kernstown. The Confederates were defeated but because of the attack more Northern troops were sent into the Valley, thus weakening the army being readied for a march on Richmond. Although the battle was lost, the Confederates won a strategic victory. Mathew Brady made a picture from this exact spot.

THE WILDERNESS . . . When Grant tried to cut between Lee and Richmond, Lee struck hard at the Federal army in the Wilderness. The first phase of the battle took place in this area. For two days, May 5 and 6, the armies were locked in a vicious struggle, but neither succeeded in achieving its objective of destroying the other. They then moved toward the southeast where the battle of Spotsylvania Courthouse was fought.

CUMBERLAND GAP—GAINES' MILL . . . Confederate forces occupied Cumberland Gap, top, until September, 1863, when they were captured by Gen. Ambrose E. Burnside. The Battle of Gaines' Mill was fought on the third day of the Seven Days Battles. These developed when Gen. George B. McClellan's Army of the Potomac moved on Richmond, defended by the Army of Northern Virginia, now commanded by Gen. Robert E. Lee.

CHICKAHOMINY . . . In the peninsula campaign, McClellan landed his army at Fortress Monroe on the tip of the peninsula between the York and James rivers and moved toward Richmond. In late June, 1862, he had one corps north of the Chickahominy River, the other four corps on the south side. Lee attacked the isolated corps. This was the beginning of the Seven Days Battles.

WHITE OAK SWAMP . . . One of the major obstacles to military movement around Richmond were the swamps and marshes. This is White Oak Swamp which lies between the Chickahominy and the James. In the Seven Days Battles, the Confederate army numbered 85,000, the Union army over 100,000. Yet Lee managed to maintain the offensive and remove the threat to Richmond.

HARPERS FERRY . . . The view of Harpers Ferry was made from Maryland Heights. On the left are Loudoun Heights, Va., and the Shenandoah River. The Potomac is in the foreground. Harpers Ferry was the scene of the John Brown Raid in 1859. Brown, an ardent abolitionist and fanatic, conceived a plan to liberate the slaves and set up a Negro stronghold in the mountains. He chose Harpers Ferry because it was near the Mason-Dixon line and at the head of the Shenandoah Valley while the mountains of Virginia offered a convenient hiding place. The raid began on October 16. Brown and his men barricaded themselves in the arsenal, which stood near the railroad bridge and depot in the right foreground. Later they took refuge in the Federal armory's engine house, which was attacked by a group of Marines that came from Washington with Col. Robert E. Lee and Lt. J. E. B. ("Jeb") Stuart. Brown was injured and ten of his men killed. Since Harpers Ferry was then still part of Virginia, Brown was indicted for treason against Virginia and for "conspiring with slaves to commit treason and murder." He was brought to trial in nearby Charles Town, convicted and hanged. Harpers Ferry changed hands many times during the Civil War. Its capture in 1862 by Stonewall Jackson was a prelude to Sharpsburg. Right, the Catoctin Mountains near Lucketts, Va. Jackson moved his troops through this beautiful country on his way into Maryland in early September, 1862.

165

FREDERICKSBURG . . . After Burnside assumed command of the Army of the Potomac, he launched an attack on Fredericksburg. The plan was to move his army of 120,-000 across the Rappahannock on pontoons and seize Marye's Heights, below, which was behind the city. At the bottom of the heights were a sunken road and a stone wall, above. With incredible bravery, Union infantrymen assaulted Marye's Heights fourteen times. They came within 25 yards of the wall, but could go no further. After losing 12,600 men, the beaten Union forces retreated north across the Rappahannock.

SALEM CHURCH . . . Built in 1844, this church is one of the principal landmarks of the Chancellorsville battlefield. It is southwest of Fredericksburg on Rt. 3. At Chancellorsville the last and most daring of all the Lee-Jackson maneuvers took place. Lee divided his small force (already split once before) in face of an army much larger than his, and in a dramatic fashion won a victory in the face of an apparent defeat. Chancellorsville is really three battles, and the Confederates won two of them. The total losses were about 17,000 for the Union army and some 13,000 for the Confederates.

MEETING PLACE . . . This is along the Orange Plank Road where Lee and Jackson bivouacked before the Battle of Chancellorsville and met for the last time. At the meeting on May 1, 1863, they planned the battle, one of the most daringly conceived engagements of the war. The next morning Jackson moved out on the bold maneuver that again divided the Confederate army. To get there on time Jackson made the most famous of all his marches. At right, the monument marks the spot where Jackson fell mortally wounded about 9 P.M. on May 2, 1863 by the mistaken fire of his own men. He died eight days later.

STONEWALL JACKSON . . . The heroic equestrian statue of Stonewall Jackson marks the spot where he got his famous nickname during the first battle of Manassas. When Gen. Barnard E. Bee saw Jackson's troops standing firm, awaiting the enemy attack, Bee pointed to the brigade, shouting, "Look! There stands Jackson like a stone wall! Rally behind the Virginians!" Bee's men echoed the call and formed on the Virginian colors. Stonewall Jackson had won his immortal name.

167

SECOND MANASSAS . . . In 1862 the Manassas area was the scene of another unsuccessful "On to Richmond" drive. This time Gen. John Pope was met by Lee and Jackson who had just driven the Army of the Potomac from the suburbs of Richmond. Jackson, with a flying column, went around Pope's right flank and destroyed the Federal supply base at Manassas Junction. After the two-day battle, the Union army retired within the Washington defenses. It had lost some 14,000 men; Lee's losses were around 10,000.

BRANDY STATION . . . The battle of Brandy Station, fought on June 9, 1863, was the biggest cavalry battle of the war. About 10,000 were on each side in this northern Virginia engagement which was fought in the classic cavalry manner with stirrup-to-stirrup charges. Brandy Station is significant because here, for the first time, Federal cavalry held its own against the usually superior Confederates. The North's good showing helped them in succeeding encounters.

WILDERNESS CHURCH . . . The Wilderness battlefield is about 17 miles west of Fredericksburg in the heart of a heavily wooded area, thick underbrush and deep ravines, relieved only by a few scattered clearings. Because of the ruggedness of the terrain, the battle was fought along three main roads. Wilderness Baptist Church is on the Orange Turnpike, one of the three. This was the first battle in which Gen. U. S. Grant was commander of all northern forces. Here he launched the campaign that was to win the war.

CROSS KEYS . . . In June Federal forces pursued Jackson in two columns. One division of Jackson's army held off one column at Cross Keys. The next day Jackson defeated the other column in the Battle of Port Republic. Orders transferring Federal elements from the Valley were again cancelled. None of the Northern troops that had fought against Jackson in these engagements ever did reach the Army of the Potomac.

BLOODY ANGLE . . . On the west face of the Confederate salient at Spotsylvania—thereafter known as the Bloody Angle—was fought on May 12, 1864 one of the most savagely contested hand-to-hand engagements of the war. The men fired at point-blank range and then bayoneted and clubbed one another across the logs of the parapet. The fighting began at 6 A.M. and lasted until nearly 3 o'clock the next morning when the Confederates withdrew.

SPOTSYLVANIA . . . After failing to defeat Lee in the Wilderness, Grant moved eastward to Spotsylvania, 10 miles southwest of Fredericksburg, in an effort to get between Lee and Richmond. After finding Lee ahead of him, he attacked several times. Here for the first time in America field fortifications were fully developed. Musketry fire was so intense that it cut down whole trees; one oak was 22 inches in diameter. Three days after the fierce and bloody battle, Grant directed his army in a great flanking movement toward Richmond.

COLD HARBOR . . . Grant prepared to deliver an annihilating assault at Cold Harbor, a strategic crossroads guarding the approaches of Richmond. The Union army's hopeless attack against Lee's well-entrenched troops lasted less than 30 minutes but it left over 7,000 killed and wounded. The area is still marked with trenches. The Battle of Cold Harbor saved Richmond for another ten months, but it was Lee's last major victory. Grant then moved by his left flank over the James in a quick attempt to take Petersburg.

THE CRATER . . . During the siege of Petersburg, members of a Pennsylvania regiment, many of them coal miners, dug a tunnel to a Confederate battery directly opposite them. It took them about a month to dig the 511-foot tunnel and the lateral galleries. On July 30, 1864, they exploded four tons of powder. The explosion blew up the Confederate battery and left a crater about 170 feet long, 60 feet wide and 30 feet deep. Union troops occupied the crater but the Confederates soon regained possession.

THE DICTATOR . . . Also known as the Petersburg Express, this 13-inch 17,-000-pound mortar was used by the Union army to shell Petersburg from a distance of two and one-half miles. From the summer of 1864 to the spring of 1865, Lee and Grant engaged in a struggle which took place in a semi-circle around Petersburg, and covered about 170 square miles, the largest single battlefield of the war. Petersburg was the supply funnel for Richmond (23 miles to the north), the Confederate government, and Lee's Army of Northern Virginia.

FORT FISHER . . . By October 2, 1864, Union forces had won the ground where they subsequently built Fort Fisher, one of the largest earth forts ever erected in North America. Here Grant's army was only three miles from the last railroad running into Petersburg. The North had possession of the other four. It was from Fort Fisher that Grant on April 2, 1865 launched his final assault.

FORT STEDMAN . . . By mid-March of 1865, the climax of the campaign was close at hand. In a major diversionary effort to withdraw from Richmond and Petersburg with the 50,000 troops he had left, Lee ordered an attack on the Union lines at Fort Stedman. The attack was made on March 25, and it failed. The Confederates lost more than 4,000 killed, wounded and captured. Union casualties were less than 1,500.

THE JAMES . . . The siege of Petersburg was punctuated in September, 1864, when Grant slipped two corps back across the James to attack Forts Gilmer and Harrison, two strongly fortified positions in the Richmond defenses. Fort Gilmer resisted the assault, but Fort Harrison was captured and renamed Fort Burnham. To protect their position, Union forces also constructed Fort Brady. Much of the activity took place in this vicinity.

APPOMATTOX . . . After Lee's lines crumbled at Petersburg, Richmond fell and Lee retreated toward Lynchburg. On Sunday, April 9, 1865, Lee's army was surrounded at Appomattox Courthouse. A flag of truce was sent out and informal conferences were held. Then Grant and Lee, accompanied by members of their staffs, met in the McLean House, on the right, at the edge of the village. Here the surrender of the Confederate force was negotiated. The four-year Civil War was all but ended.

BALL'S BLUFF . . . On the Virginia side of the Potomac, a mile north of Leesburg on Rt. 15, is Ball's Bluff. Here on October 21, 1861, a Union force attempted to climb the nearly 100-foot river bank. They suffered 921 casualties, nearly half their force. The Confederates lost 129 from some 1,200 men. A Congressional investigation committee termed the engagement "the most atrocious military blunder in history." There are 25 Union graves in the cemetery. All are unidentified except the center stone. This is No. 13 and bears the name of James Allen of Massachusetts. Ball's Bluff is the smallest national military cemetery in the United States.

ACKNOWLEDGMENTS

I suppose it has been well over 30 years since the charm of Virginia began to cast a spell over me as a photographer, because it has been that long ago assignments in the Tidewater area began to fall my way for the Baltimore *Sunday Sun.* In between I have spent many days and traveled many miles to get the portrait of a great Commonwealth presented in these pages. As a result literally hundreds of people have helped make this book possible. But I can only thank those *in absentia.*

Associates who worked side by side to produce this volume require special acknowledgment. The captain of our crew, Stanley L. Cahn, put all the pieces together and kept us in line to the very end. Harold A. Williams, editor of the *Sunday Sun,* contributed the lucid and interesting captions, and kept his keen eyes peeled in the choice of pictures. And the wonderful assistance of Virginius Dabney, author of the introduction and editor of the text, was inspiring. This famous historian and journalist has made an invaluable contribution.

Due credit must be given to Gaylord Lee Clark, who was largely responsible for my picturing Virginia and helped make the many contacts needed. The help of Robert Burgess, Howard M. Smith, John Melville Jennings and Hervey Brackbill was also appreciated.

Mechanically, this volume has had the same meticulous care by J. Albert Caldwell and his son Jack as they lavished on my previous three books. Employing their amazing process of Unitone lithography, the Caldwells and their crew have made of my work a joy to look at.

My appreciation extends to William F. Schmick, Jr., president of the A. S. Abell Company, publisher of the *Sunpapers,* for permission to use many of the photographs that appeared in these newspapers.

Finally, my loving thanks to my patient wife, Nancy, for the scores of week-ends she allowed me to travel, winter and summer, to put this book together.   A. A. B.

INDEX